World-Class Puzzles
from the
World Puzzle Championships

Volume 4

Edited by Will Shortz and Nick Baxter

**Random House
Puzzles & Games**

Random House Puzzles & Games Web site address:
www.puzzlesatrandom.com

World Puzzle Championship/Team USA Web site address:
wpc.puzzles.com

Manufactured in the United States of America

2 4 6 8 9 7 5 3 1

First Edition

CONTENTS

CONTENTS

FOREWORD

Team USA
Zack Butler, Roger Barkan, Nick Baxter (captain),
Ron Osher, Wei-Hwa Huang

Winning Teams and Runners-up
1992–2001
1992	USA, Argentina
1993	Czech Republic, USA
1994	Czech Republic, USA
1995	USA, Czech Republic
1996	USA, Czech Republic
1997	Czech Republic, USA
1998	USA, Japan
1999	USA, Netherlands
2000	USA, Netherlands
2001	USA, Czech Republic

Winning Individuals 1992–2001
1992	David Samuel (Canada)
1993	Robert Babilon (Czech Republic)
1994	Ron Osher (USA)
1995	Wei-Hwa Huang (USA)
1996	Robert Babilon (Czech Republic)
1997	Wei-Hwa Huang (USA)
1998	Wei-Hwa Huang (USA)
1999	Wei-Hwa Huang (USA)
2000	Ulrich Voigt (Germany)
2001	Ulrich Voigt (Germany)

Every year since 1992, some of the world's most creative puzzling has taken place at the World Puzzle Championship.

For example, at the 2001 WPC in Brno, Czech Republic, the organizers staged a fashion show in which a series of ten models, each sporting a distinctive outfit, walked a runway. Afterward, the contestants—more than 100 of them from 21 countries—had to match the clothing items with the models who wore them.

Another event was, in effect, a three-card monte game, but with real people acting out a "slightly" strange challenge. A document was placed in one of six identical attaché cases. Actors dressed as spies then secretly exchanged the cases on stage. The contestants were asked to identify the spy holding the original document at the end.

We can't reproduce the above challenges within the pages of this book. However, we have gathered for you some of the cleverest and most interesting pencil-and-paper puzzles from the championship. As always, the puzzles are language- and culture-neutral (for example, no crosswords or other standard word puzzles), so that people from all countries can compete equally.

We're also presenting the entire 2001 U.S./Canada Qualifying Test, which was used to select members of these countries' respective teams. You can take the test under timed conditions to see how you would stack up in real competition . . . or else solve just the puzzles you want at a more leisurely pace. The choice is yours.

We'd like to thank Vitězslav Koudelka and his team of puzzlemakers in the Czech Republic for providing the puzzles used in the championship. Team USA would also like to thank the companies whose financial support helps make our participation possible: Binary Arts, the innovative puzzle catalog company; Random House, which regularly publishes these collections of WPC puzzles; and Games magazine and its sister publication, Games World of Puzzles.

To try out for the U.S. or Canadian team in a future WPC, or simply to get more information, please visit the website for the U.S. Team (wpc.puzzles.com) or the World Puzzle Federation (www.worldpuzzle.org).

—Will Shortz and Nick Baxter

U.S. AND CANADIAN TEAM QUALIFYING TEST

For the third straight year, the U.S. and Canadian Team Qualifying Test was administered via the Internet. Up for grabs were positions on the U.S. and Canadian teams that would compete in the upcoming World Puzzle Championship.

Contestants downloaded the test instructions a day in advance so they could familiarize themselves with what they were to face (similar to the procedure used during the WPC itself). Then on a Saturday in June at precisely 16:00 GMT, contestants received the complete test and embarked on a 2½-hour adventure in competitive puzzle solving.

This year the top U.S. spot was contested in a virtual cyber-duel. Two solvers, Roger Barkan and Jonathan Rivet, both distanced themselves from the rest of the pack, each solving an improbable 25 of 26 problems. But it was Roger, on the strength of solving the most difficult final problem, who emerged with more points, earning himself the coveted position on the U.S. team.

The top Canadian solver was Derek Kisman, solving 17 of 24 problems. The test was also available to anyone around the world who was interested. Top solvers from outside North America were David McNeill of Ireland (265) and Niels Roest of the Netherlands (260).

The Qualifying Test is presented here in its entirety. You can choose to take your time and solve the problems at your leisure—or, if you're ready to match wits with the qualifiers listed here, set your stopwatch for 2½ hours and dig in! As always, the problems get harder as you go along (you'll find the point values with the solutions). But don't guess, since incorrect answers incur a 5-point penalty.

As always, good luck and have fun!

U.S. Qualifying Scores

1	Roger Barkan	320
2	Jonathan Rivet	305
3	Stephen Wang	285
4	Scott Purdy	255
5	Andrew Brecher	255
6	Alan Lemm	250
7	Randy Rogers	240
8	Richard Dunlap	235
9	Joseph DeVincentis	230
10	George Tolley	225

Canadian Qualifying Scores

1	Derek Kisman	250
2	Byron Calver	215
3	Nicholas McHaffie	200
4	Bradley Bart	195
5	Eric Sutherland	185
6	Trevor Green	185
7	Darren Rigby	175
8	Ian Goldberg	165
9	David Savitt	155
10	Gary Sherman	130

GREAT DIVIDE

Paint 10 squares black so that the 5 x 6 unit rectangle below is divided into two pieces:
one black and the other white, each with the same size and shape.

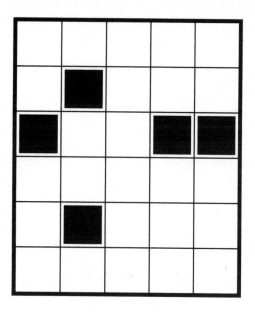

NUMBER BOXES

Place the digits 1 through 9 (each used exactly once) into the circles,
so that the numbers inside every rectangle have the same sum.

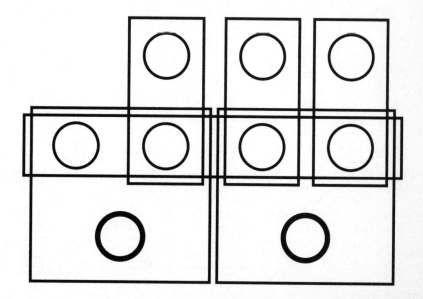

BIRDIE FOR THE BEAR

Which of the numbered drawings matches the drawing in the upper left?

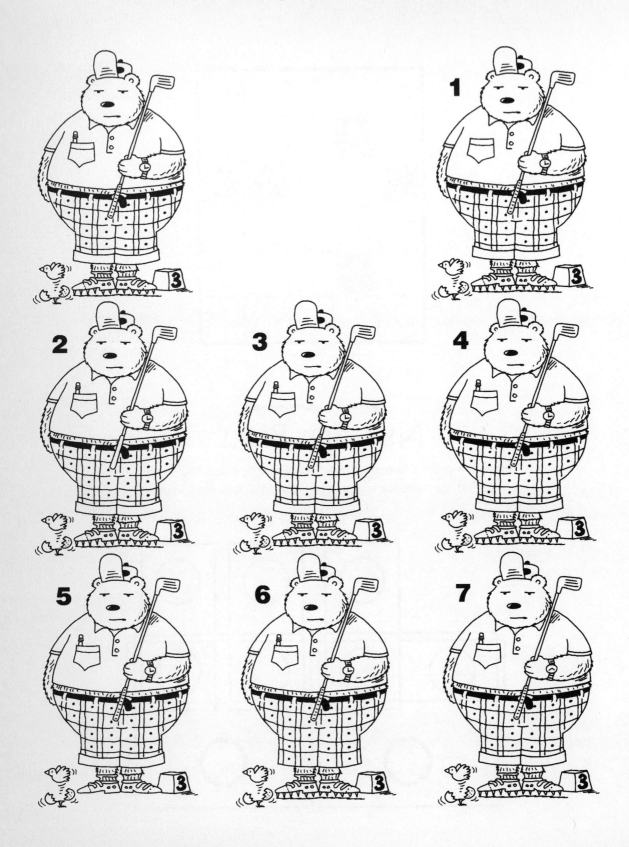

COMMON TOUCH

In each of these puzzles, the seven geographical names in the Yes group all share a simple
but unusual property that none of the six names in the No group have. For each puzzle,
pick one of the eight names from the Name List at the right that shares the property of the Yes group.
(Note: The unusual properties are all word-related, and have nothing to do with the locations themselves;
i.e., no knowledge of geography is needed to solve the puzzles.)

1

Yes	No
Bordeaux, France	Bristol, England
Glasgow, Scotland	Caracas, Venezuela
Hangzhou, China	Khartoum, Sudan
Jericho, Jordan	Omsk, Russia
Juneau, United States	Perth, Australia
Montevideo, Uruguay	Seoul, Korea
Tokyo, Japan	

Name List:
Alma-Ata, Kazakhstan
Chinju, Korea
Ciudad del Este, Paraguay
Damascus, Syria
Kérouané, Guinea
Kuala Lumpur, Malaysia
Odense, Denmark
Stowe, United States

2

Yes	No
El Tigre, Venezuela	Apia, Samoa
Kaffrine, Senegal	Bujumbura, Burundi
Nandi, Fiji	Calcutta, India
Ottawa, Canada	Kingston, Jamaica
Sincelejo, Colombia	Lilongwe, Malawi
Villa Sanjurjo, Morocco	Malmö, Sweden
Yokohama, Japan	

3

Yes	No
Arlon, Belgium	Bulawayo, Zimbabwe
Borujerd, Iran	Moma, Mozambique
Burgdorf, Switzerland	Oulu, Finland
Corumbé, Brazil	Quan Long, Vietnam
Lvov, Ukraine	Tegucigalpa, Honduras
Moulins, France	Temuco, Chile
Tuxtla, Mexico	

MISSING DOMINOES

Twenty-six dominoes in a standard set of 28 dominoes (double-0 through double-6) have been placed in the tray shown below. The domino halves are indicated by digits from 0 to 6, corresponding to the number of pips; but the dominoes' borders are not shown in the tray. Which two dominoes are missing?

0	3	6	5	2	6	4	0	5	6	2	5	1
3	0	0	4	1	1	6	1	3	0	0	4	2
4	6	3	5	4	0	1	1	1	6	2	4	1
3	6	2	2	4	2	6	4	5	0	3	2	5

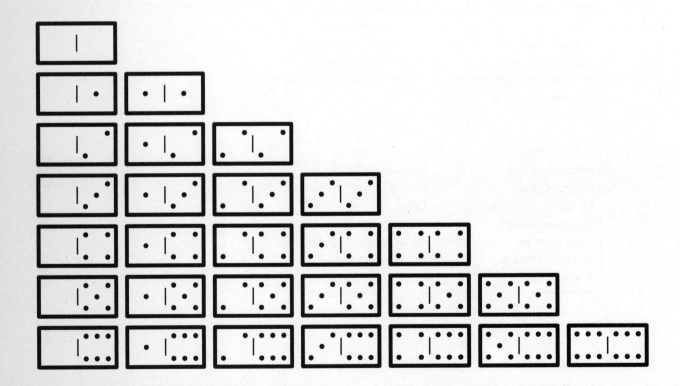

DOMINO STACKING

You are given the set of ten dominoes shown below the diagram. Replace the domino halves with digits from 0 to 4, corresponding to the number of pips; then place this set into the diagram so that each digit is different from the horizontally adjacent digits (if any) and larger than the one below it (if any).

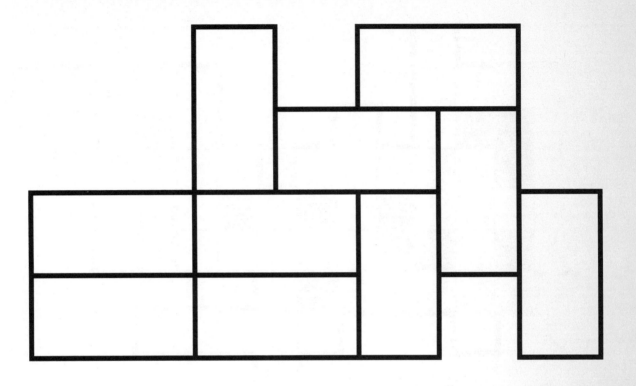

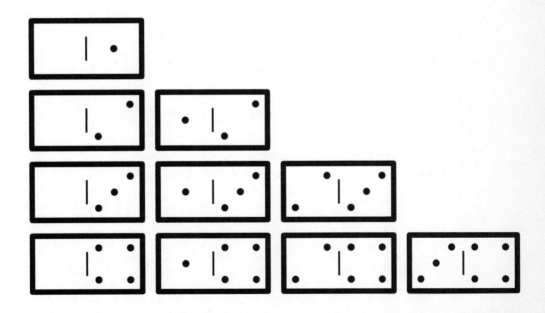

CRISSCROSS

Fifteen of the Czech animal names below can be placed in the grid to complete the crisscross pattern across and down. Which name is left over when you're done? Note: diacritical marks *are* significant. For example, a C with a hacek (Č) can cross another C only if it also has a hacek.

BIZON (bison)   MAKAK (macaque)

BŮVOL (buffalo)   MEZEK (mule)

GIBON (gibbon)   MORČE (guinea pig)

JELEN (deer)   OKAPI (okapi)

KOALA (koala)   OPICE (ape)

KOČKA (cat)   PAKŮÓ (wildebeest)

KRTEK (mole)   PRASE (pig)

LEMUR (lemur)   TČHOR (skunk)

BATTLESHIPS

Locate the position of the 10-ship fleet in the grid. The fleet is shown to the right of the grid: one 4-unit battleship, two 3-unit cruisers, three 2-unit destroyers and four 1-unit submarines. Each segment of a ship occupies a single cell. Ships are oriented either horizontally or vertically, and they do not touch each other, not even diagonally. The numbers along the right and bottom edges of the grid indicate the total number of the ship segments that appear in the respective rows and columns.

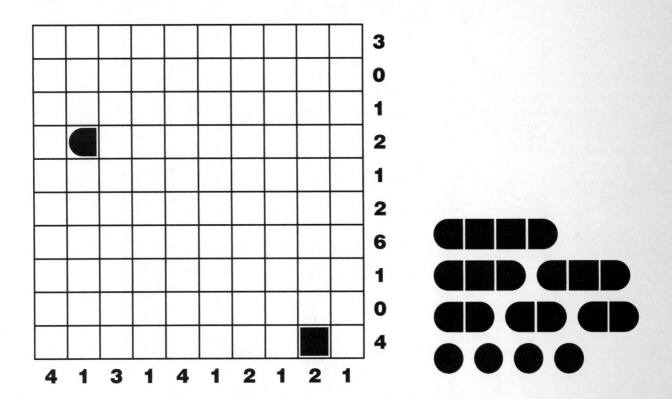

END VIEW

Enter the letters A, B, C and D once in each row and column. The clues outside the grid indicate which letter appears first from that direction. For example, B must be the topmost letter in the left column.

	B		D	D	C			
D								A
D								C
B								
								C
B								C
				C		C		

SUM PLACE

If the following are true relationships:

PANAMA + JAPAN = 5
FIJI + CUBA = 7
SWEDEN + NORWAY = 9
AUSTRIA + AUSTRALIA = 7

Then what is the corresponding value for:

CANADA + UNITED STATES = ?

LOOP-D-LOOP

Trace a path from the upper left square back to itself, jumping to each of the other squares exactly once. Each jump can be any distance, but must be in the direction indicated in the current square.

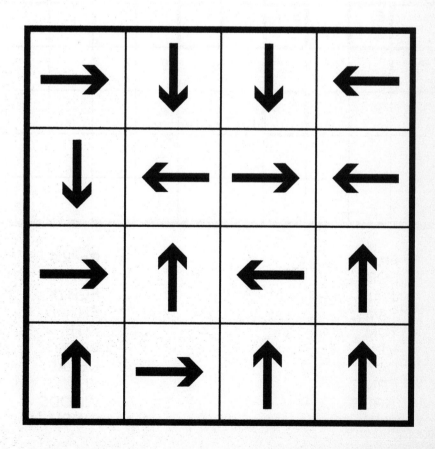

CLUB SANDWICH

The first and last names of nine professional golfers are to be wedged into the grid below, crisscross-style (that is, words are completely interlocked and go from left to right or top to bottom, and no words of two or more letters not in the list of names are formed in the completed grid). Each first name ("Front 9") *begins* on a numbered square, and each last name ("Back 9") *ends* on a numbered square; the number in the square is the number of letters in the corresponding name.

Front 9
BOB
JIM
SAM
TOM
MIKE
DAVID
ERNIE
TIGER
VIJAY

Back 9
TWAY
FURYK
SNEAD
KITE
WEIR
DUVAL
ELS
WOODS
SINGH

RAILROAD TRACKS

Lay a single, closed loop of railroad track that travels through each square of the grid exactly once. The track connects squares horizontally or vertically, and crosses itself only at the six crossings ("+") shown in the grid. The track does not turn as it passes through the stations, which are the squares containing numbers. As you follow the track, visit stations 1 through 5 in order, then return to station 1.

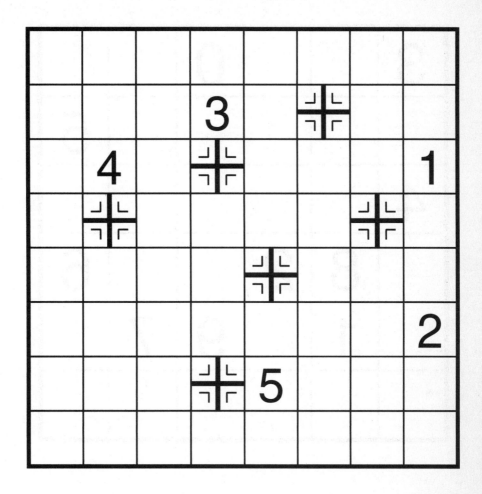

50/50 MINESWEEPER

Exactly half of the squares in the diagram below contain a mine. Additionally, exactly half of the numbered squares also contain mines. A number in a square *without* a mine is the correct count of the mines in the horizontally, vertically, and diagonally adjacent squares; a number in a square *with* a mine is *not* the correct count of the mines in adjacent squares. Where are the mines?

3			0		
					5
4					
	8	2			6
	1		9	7	

ALICE MAZE

Alice starts chasing rabbits at the upper left corner ("S") of the maze. Her goal is the rabbit hole in the lower-right corner ("F"). She begins moving one unit at a time, in a straight line either horizontally or vertically, but only in the direction of the arrow(s) in the current square. When she lands on a square with a "+"-pill, the distance of all future moves is increased by one unit; when she lands on a square with a "–"-pill, the distance of all future moves is decreased by one unit. Alice cannot move past the edge of the maze.

As an example, here is a poor way to start the maze: move one square down, one square right, then one square down. Alice landed on a square with a "–"-pill. All future moves are of length zero, which means she's stuck.

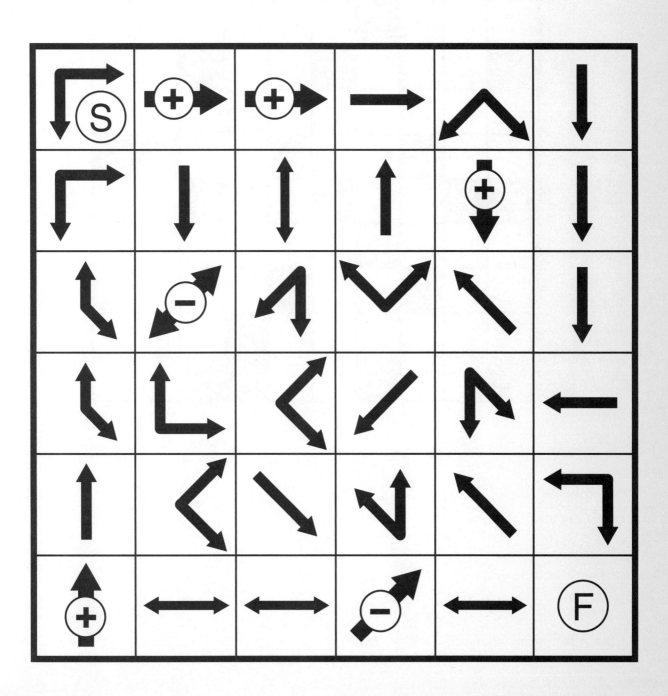

CROSS SUMS VARIATION

This is a standard Cross Sums puzzle, a crossword made with numbers instead of words, but with one exception. Enter a single digit from 1 to 9 into each empty square so that the sum of the digits in each Across answer equals the value given to the left. In this variation, the sum for each Down answer is *always 15.* No digit is repeated within a single answer.

BAD MATH

In the following long division problem, change each of the digits to a different digit so that the arithmetic is correct. Note that there is no remainder, and that numbers do not start with leading zeros.

```
          4321
      ┌────────
  15 )  95867
       42
       ──
        365
         12
         ──
          72
          69
          ──
```

RETROGRADE BATTLESHIPS

Place the entire fleet into the grid as you would in classic Battleships.
In this variation, the possible placements of the ships are given; the puzzle is to find the correct subset.

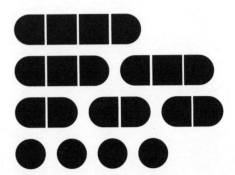

TOTALLY BATTLESHIPS

Place the entire fleet into the grid as you would in classic Battleships. In this variation,
the numbers along the bottom and right edges of the grid indicate the sum of the numbers
in each of the ship segments that appear in each respective column or row.

5	5	5	7	5	9	1	7	3	1	**1**
9	9	9	9	4	3	3	3	4	2	**3**
6	7	8	7	5	5	9	6	6	4	**30**
9	2	7	5	9	5	7	7	7	3	**9**
6	2	1	5	5	1	1	4	8	6	**20**
5	5	5	5	3	1	2	2	8	8	**5**
7	6	4	4	8	1	3	3	9	1	**15**
2	5	8	1	3	8	1	1	8	2	**5**
6	9	4	5	6	3	5	9	4	3	**3**
7	5	9	2	8	4	5	1	4	1	**4**
15	**5**	**13**	**7**	**5**	**4**	**8**	**7**	**27**	**4**	

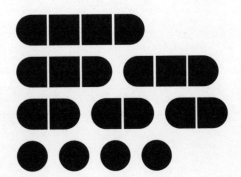

22

HAVE SUM FUN!

Place a different digit from 1 to 9 inside each of the nine triangles so that each of the four circled numbers is the sum of the digits in the triangles that touch it.

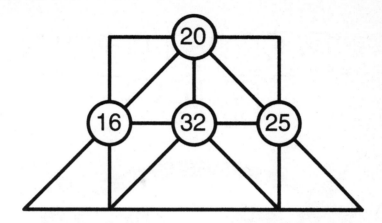

HIGH FIVE

You have a set of five numbers. When adding together each of the ten possible pairs, you get the following sums:

0, 6, 11, 12, 17, 20, 23, 26, 32, 37.

What are the five original numbers?

Arrowheading

In this maze, your course headings are predetermined and point values have been assigned to each passage. Starting from the bottom intersection, travel to each of the other five intersections and return to the beginning intersection with the *lowest* possible total score (the sum of the values for each passage used).

MEANDERING RIVER

The names of 25 world rivers can be found in the word search grid.
Each name reads in a straight line horizontally, vertically or diagonally.
The 30 empty spaces in the grid must be filled in before the puzzle can be completed.

```
K T E C N E R W A L T S
G       O V E D V N R H
E E N S   E E L A   I E
O R O   T E S T   L   E
S P   R E F S S   S   L
H   E T G T       V O   I
A   M E     N A R N     D
N   S   N O N I T   S O
N   A   I R E A   H E C
O R   S V K T   U E E O
N A S U D N I E       R
N I R T Y S H U S E D C
```

CROCODILE (South Africa)

DEVON (Scotland)

DNIEPER (Russia/Belarus/Ukraine)

DNIESTER (Ukraine/Moldova)

DVINA (Russia/Belarus/Latvia)

FEATHER (USA)

GEORGINA (Australia)

ILLINOIS (USA)

INDUS (Pakistan)

IRTYSH (Kazakhstan/Russia)

KENNET (England)

MEKONG (Thailand/Laos/Vietnam)

NELSON (Canada)

NIGER (Mali/Nigeria)

ORONTES (Syria)

PECHORA (Russia)

SEINE (France)

SEMLIKI (Zaire/Uganda)

SHANNON (Ireland)

ST. CLAIR (USA)

ST. LAWRENCE (Canada)

TENNESSEE (USA)

TIGRIS (Iraq)

VLTAVA (Czech Republic)

YUKON (Canada/USA)

FENCES VARIATION

Draw a single continuous loop by connecting neighboring dots horizontally or vertically (but not diagonally). A numbered square indicates exactly how many of its four, or eight, edges are used by the path.

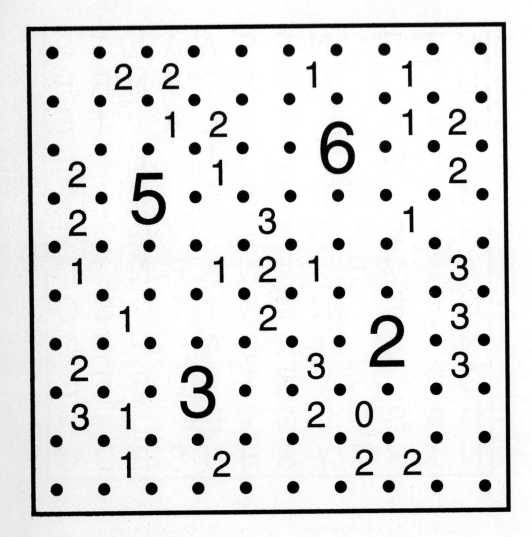

THE TENTH WORLD PUZZLE CHAMPIONSHIP

The 10th World Puzzle Championship was held in Brno, Czech Republic, October 8-14, 2001. With an appropriate theme of "2001: A Puzzle Odyssey," contestants were treated to an eclectic selection of traditional pencil-and-paper, manipulative, and innovative stage-acting puzzles (as described in the Foreword on page 5).

After three days and 15 rounds of intense solving, Team USA emerged victorious for the fourth year

Team USA
Clockwise from left: Ron Osher, Wei-Hwa Huang, Roger Barkan, and Zack Butler

Top Teams—2001	
1 USA	4,423
2 Netherlands	3,813
3 Germany	3,612
4 Hungary	3,595
5 France	3,485
6 Czech Republic	3,279
7 Poland	3,129
8 Canada	3,088
9 Belgium	2,881
10 Japan	2,565

Top Individuals—2001	
1 Ulrich Voigt (Germany)	1,469
2 Robert Babilon (Czech Republic)	1,454
3 Zack Butler (USA)	1,344
4 Wei-Hwa Huang (USA)	1,327
5 Niels Roest (Netherlands)	1,321
6 Tim Peeters (Netherlands)	1,301
7 Petr Nepovim (Czech Republic)	1,256
8 Sebastien Leroy (Belgium)	1,249
9 Derek Kisman (Canada)	1,242
10 Ron Osher (USA)	1,239
12 Roger Barkan (USA)	1,201
64 John Wetmiller (Canada)	813
83 Nicholas McHaffie (Canada)	719
90 Jan Suchanek (Canada)	613

in a row, finishing well ahead of the second-place, home team from the Czech Republic. The U.S. team was led by Zack Butler and Wei-Hwa Huang, placing third and fourth, respectively, with Ron Osher (tenth) and first-time competitor Roger Barkan (twelfth) not far behind.

Ulrich Voigt of Germany was on his own hot streak, making it two in a row himself by retaining the individual title, sneaking past former champion Robert Babilon of the Czech Republic in the final afternoon. Derek Kisman was the highest-placing Canadian, in ninth place overall.

The following pages are our favorites of the championship puzzles that can be reproduced on paper—enjoy!

WELCOME TO BRNO!

Blacken squares in the last diagram to complete the puzzle pattern.

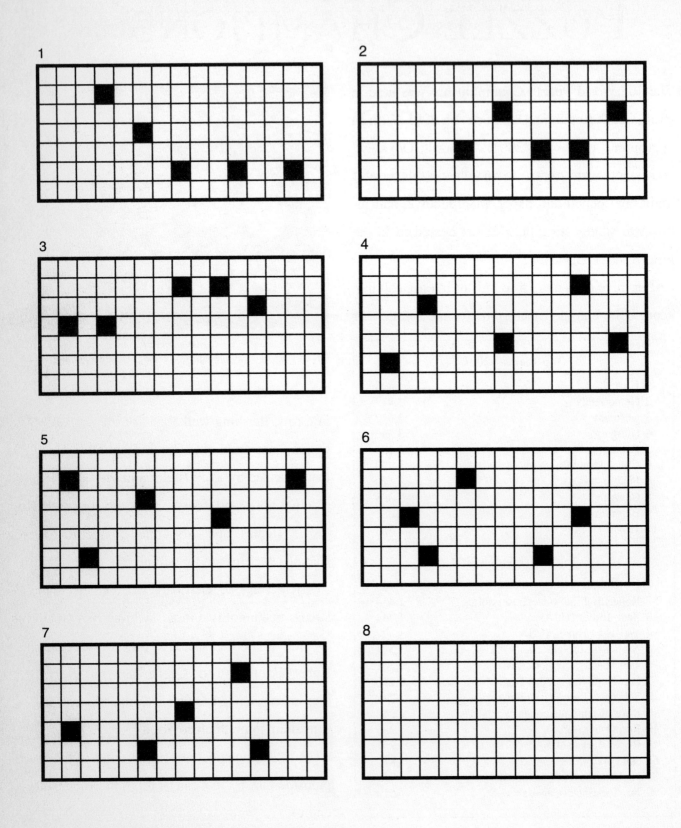

FIND THE DOGS

For each puzzle, locate all the dogs hidden in the diagram.
Dogs are formed by joining together two or more adjacent areas in the diagram.

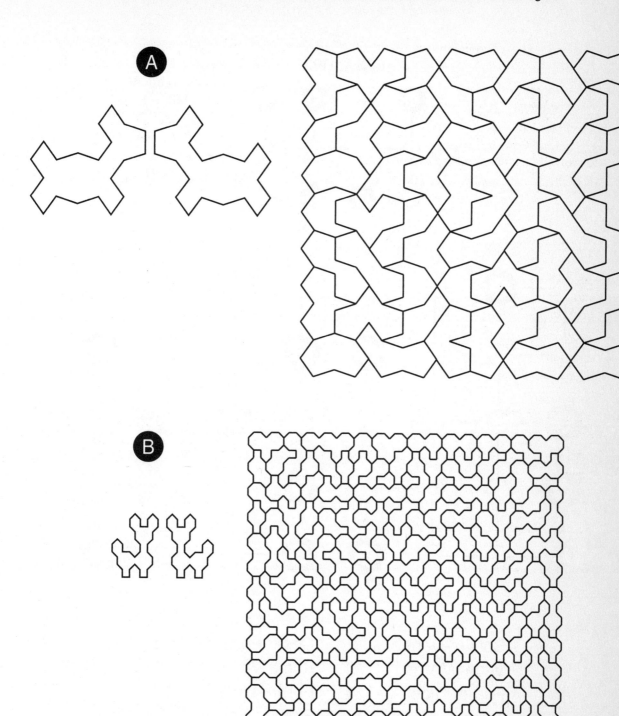

STAR TOURS

Spaceships travel among the stars (large circles with letters) and space stations (small circles) along the lines shown. The distance between selected pairs of stars is shown below. Determine the name of each lettered star.

EXAMPLE

Mur–Kor 7
Kor–Ver 3
Ver–Nir 5
Mur–Sar 5

Solution:
Kor–E
Mur–D
Nir–A
Sar–B
Ver–C

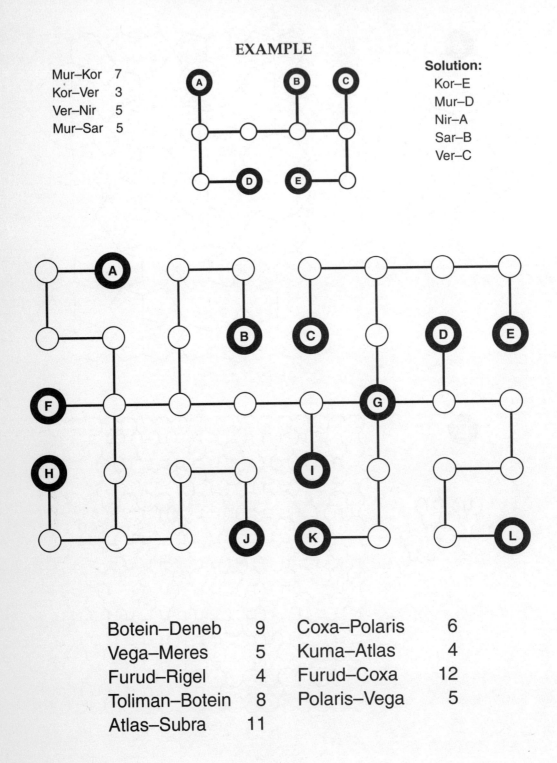

Botein–Deneb	9	Coxa–Polaris	6
Vega–Meres	5	Kuma–Atlas	4
Furud–Rigel	4	Furud–Coxa	12
Toliman–Botein	8	Polaris–Vega	5
Atlas–Subra	11		

DISTANT FUTURE

A man named JOHN lived on a distant planet. When he was 25, his son ALES was born.
After another 24 years, JOHN had a grandson called ALDY. What's interesting is that if you correctly replace the letters in the three names with numbers from 0 to 9, you obtain the years of birth of all three men.
When were JOHN, ALES and ALDY born?

MULTIPLICATION

Replace each letter with a different digit so that the indicated product is correct. In addition, the first half of the final number (the first three digits) is double the second half of this number (last three digits).

TWO x SIX = TWELVE

WORMS

Black worms inhabit a very distant planet. At each of the two sites below, there are three worms—each 12 successive squares long. The worms do not touch one another, not even diagonally, and no parts of an individual worm's body touch each other (see example). Therefore a black area of 2 x 2 cannot occur anywhere. Each number in the grid indicates how many squares are occupied by worms that neighbor that numbered square. Worms can border a square along the side or at a corner. The worms do not enter the squares with numbers. Mark the position of the three worms in each diagram.

EXAMPLE

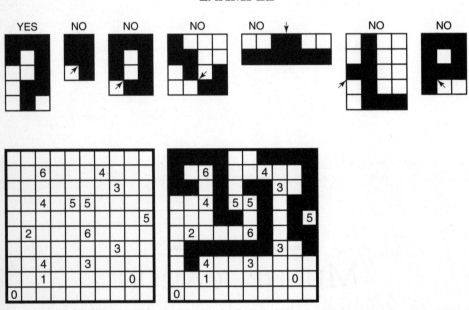

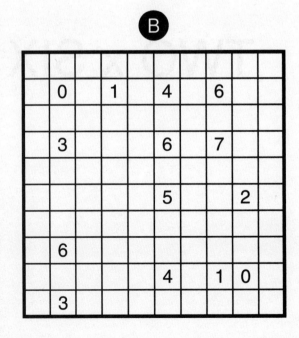

NAMES IN A TELESCOPE

First, make groups of identical shapes. Next, put the shapes in each group into numerical order. In each group, the letters that correspond to the numbers will spell out one of a group of related astronomical objects. Write these names in alphabetical order.

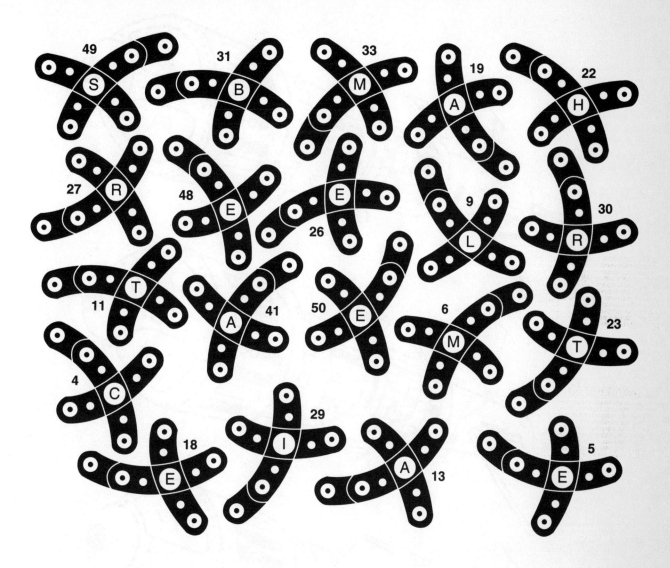

SPACESHIP

Pictured below are the plans for an original spaceship and two imitations, each differing from the original in ten details. Which plan is the original?

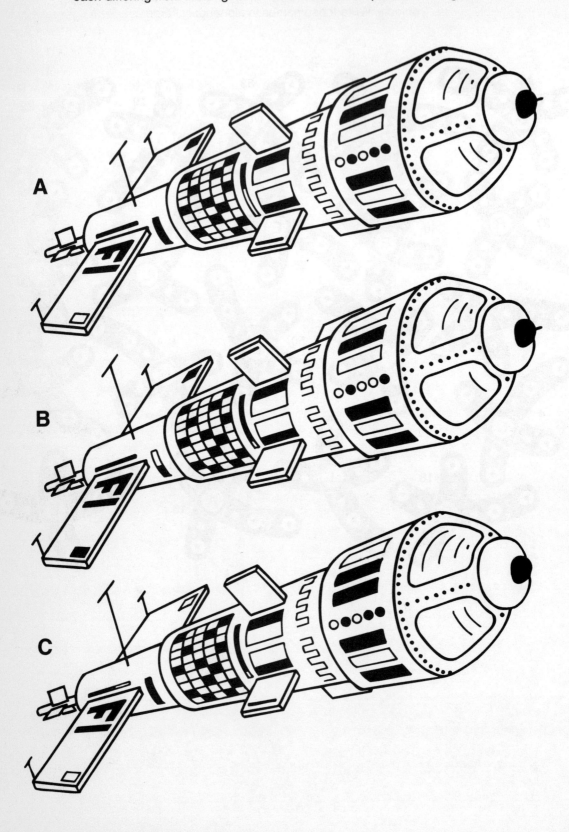

INVASION

In each puzzle, an invasion of five extraterrestrial spaceships has hit a square area. All the ships are the same shape (see illustration) and they each point in one of four possible directions: The rocket tip can only point vertically upwards or downwards, or horizontally left or right. Each spaceship consists of six segments (i.e., occupies 6 squares) and each segment-type has a different point value: The rocket tip is worth 3 points, each wing 2 points and each square of the body 1 point. Thus, the whole ship is worth 10 points. The numbers outside the diagram indicate the number of points in each row or column. Your task is to find the positions of all five spaceships. Squares with segments of two different spaceships do not touch each other, not even diagonally. Place the five spaceships into each diagram.

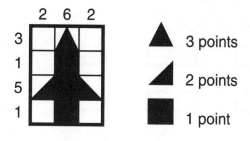

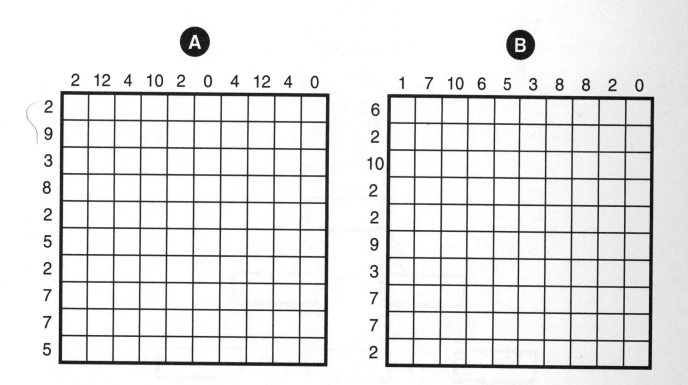

ASTEROIDS

Place the ten asteroid names into the diagram. The numbers on the connecting lines indicate how many letters the two connected asteroids have in common. Letters that appear more than once in a name count individually as independent symbols; for example, CELUTA and GALENE have three letters in common, not four.

EXAMPLE

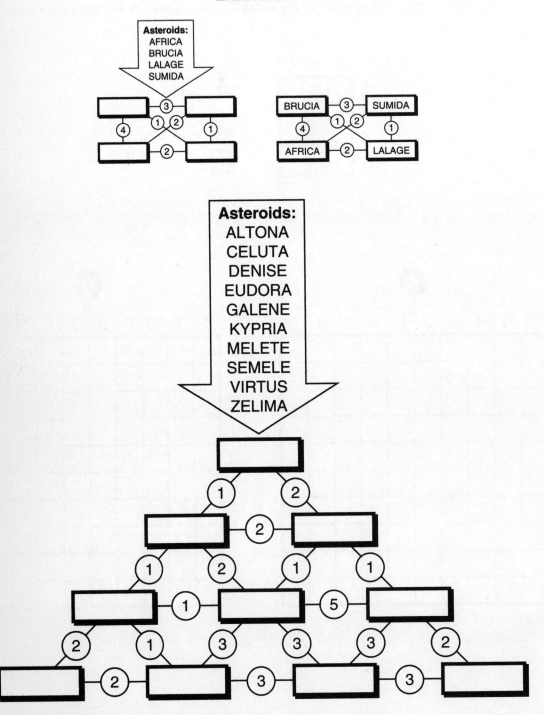

36

CONSTELLATION

Pictured below are six constellations, each with its international name. Numbers obtained by a certain logic accompany five of the six pictures. What number goes with the constellation Leo?

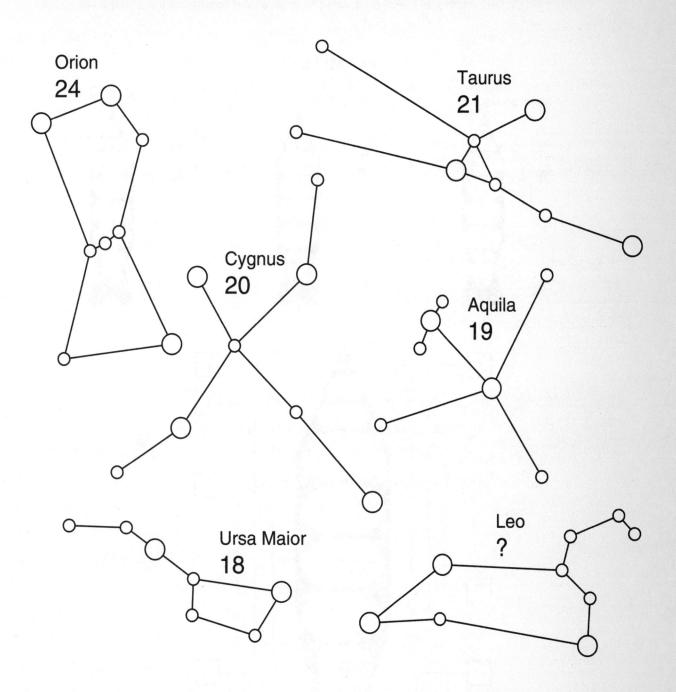

Orion
24

Taurus
21

Cygnus
20

Aquila
19

Ursa Maior
18

Leo
?

MISSION

Each of the switches A-G will change the position of the three or four hatches that it is connected to (for example, switch A controls hatches 2, 4, 7, and 8). By pressing a switch, you will open the closed hatches and close the open hatches. To start with, all hatches are shut.
Identify the smallest number of switches needed to open all the hatches at the same time.

EXAMPLE

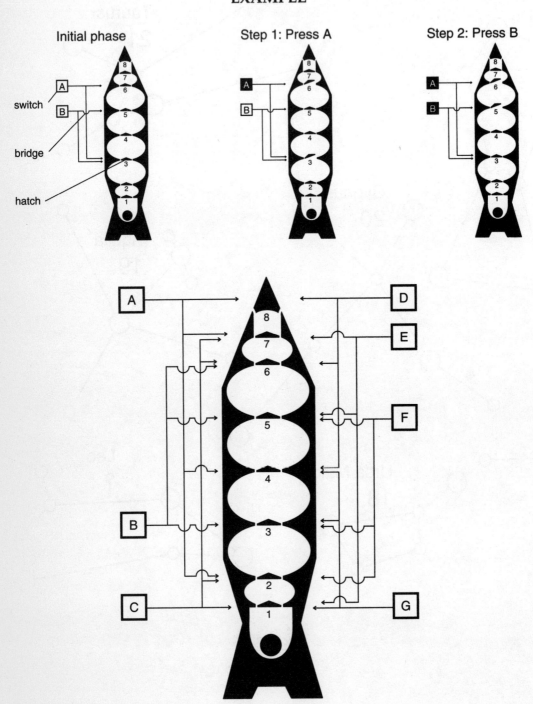

TETRAHEDRON 2001

Place the numbers 329, 331, 332, 333, 335, 337, 338 and 339 in the circles so that the sum of the six numbers on each of the four sides gives the year 2001.

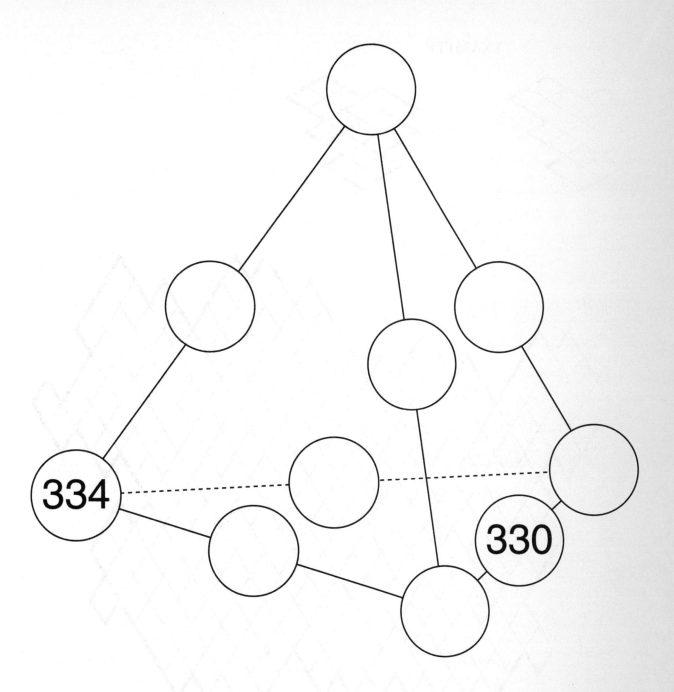

DIVIDE THE AREA

Divide the diagram into three sections of the same shape and size. The sections can be rotated, but not reflected. The dividing lines must follow along the grid lines.

EXAMPLE

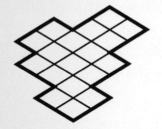 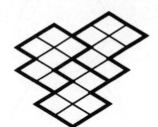

ANTIMAGIC SQUARE

Place the numbers 1 to 12 (each just once) in the 6 x 6 square so that in each row, in each column and on both main diagonals there are exactly two numbers, their totals varying between 6 and 19, each one different. Some of the totals are already provided. Fill in the numbers inside the diagram as well as the totals that are missing along the side and bottom.

EXAMPLE (for numbers 1 to 8 and totals 5 to 14)

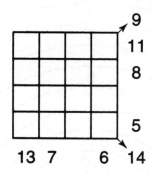

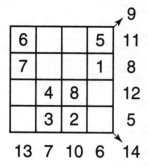

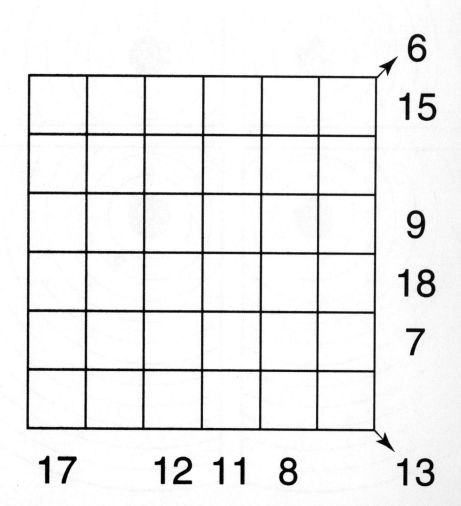

FOUR MARKSMEN

Four marksmen had a shooting competition consisting of three shots per person. Each of the 12 shots fired scored a different number of points from 1 to 13 (point values are shown on Bernard's target). At the end of the competition all four marksmen had the same total score. The diagram shows the situation after the first three shots. What were the individual scores for each of the marksmen?

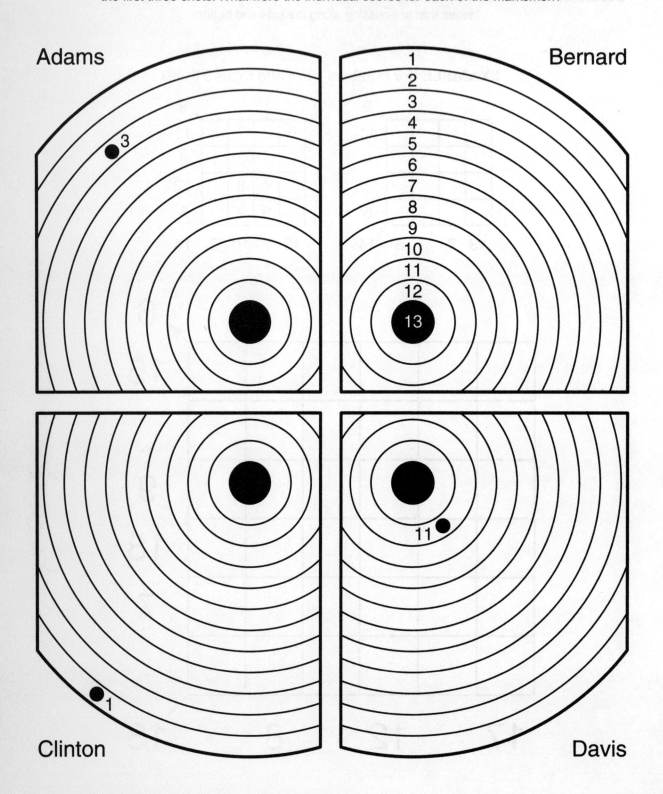

SYMBOLIC WOMEN

This puzzle is a word labyrinth: the first word is to be entered, following the direction of the arrow, into the five boxes (square or triangle) leading to the bold line. The path then turns 90 degrees and the second word is entered, ending at the next bold line. Continue in this way to the exit marked with the second arrow. Words are to be entered chain-fashion, meaning that the last letter of each word is the first letter of the next word (except for the last word at the exit). When the grid is filled in, two words not on the list but related to the title will appear in the shaded areas.

The first example diagram indicates how the path progresses. The second example diagram shows a partially completed puzzles in which the following words have been entered (in order): KIRA, AS, SOLI, IKE, ES, SILK.

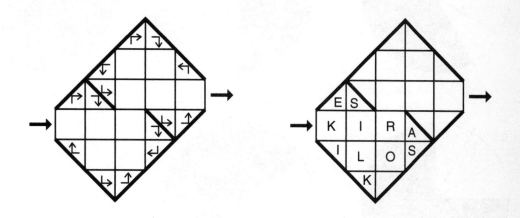

ADAM	NIELO
AERONAUT	NIEMEN
ALTIUS	NINETY
AN	NOS
AR	PEDALS
AREA	POEM
BISMARCK	RADOM
EMIL	REAP
ENTER	RENATA
ETON	SLADAR
HELP	STAB
HOLUB	SUNSET
KOREAN	TARMA
KT	TICK
LA	TINA
LASSIE	TROT
MA	TUNEL
MEDIUM	YH
MEH	

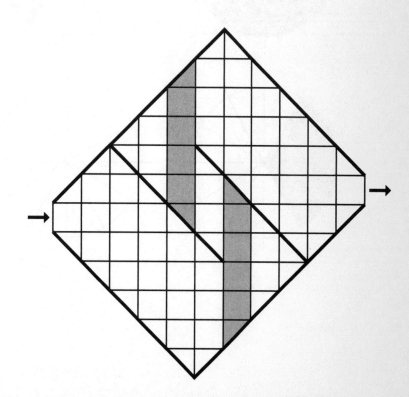

UMBRELLAS

The pictures show open umbrellas viewed from above. Fill in the appropriate areas of the umbrellas in positions B3 and C2 in such a way that the logical system is observed.

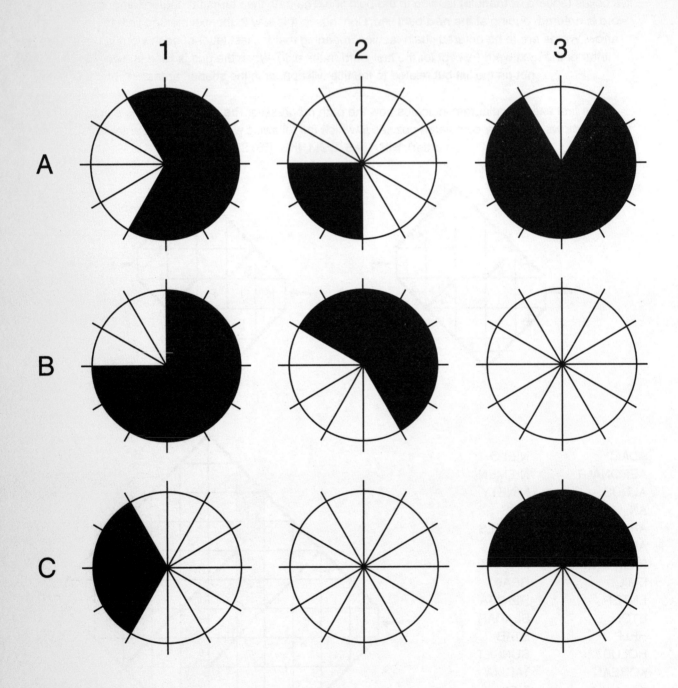

LETTER BLOCKS

Put all the blocks of the letter puzzle into the correct places in the diagram so that they fit jigsaw style.
Write each one's letter on its block. One block is already in place.

EXAMPLE

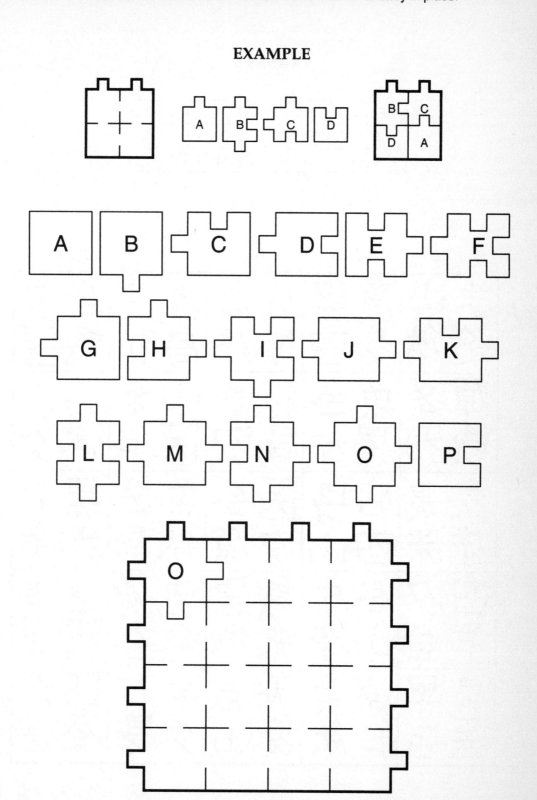

EXCHANGES

In as few moves as possible, rearrange the squares so that each of the twenty different symbols occurs exactly once in each row and each column.

EXAMPLE

	1	2	3
A	DE	FG	HJ
B	GJ	DG	EF
C	FH	EJ	DH

	1	2	3
A	DE	FG	HJ
B	GJ	DH	EF
C	FH	EJ	DG

1. B2 → C3
2. C3 → B2

COLUMNS

Place the numbers from 1 to 30 in the 30 empty sectors of the six columns below by following the indicated arithmetic operations between the pairs of adjoining sectors. This means that the number above each triangle undergoes the indicated arithmetic operation and the result is written below the triangle. Each number is to be used exactly once. The operations are: addition (+), subtraction (–), multiplication (x), and division (:).

EXAMPLE

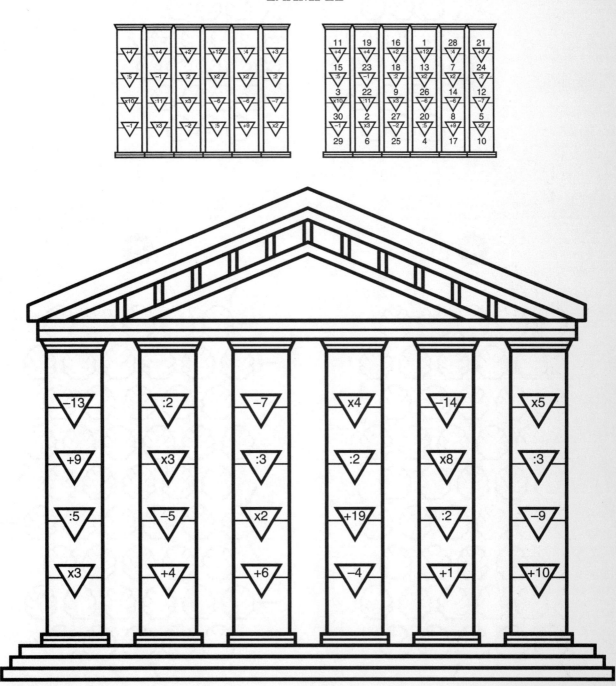

PEARLS

In each puzzle, locate the pearls hidden among the shells. Each arrow points to exactly one pearl, and each pearl is pointed to by exactly one arrow. In no case are pearls found in neighboring shells.

EXAMPLE

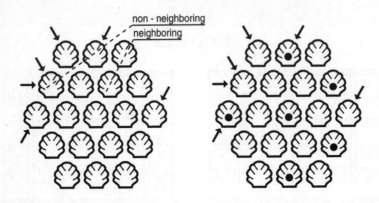

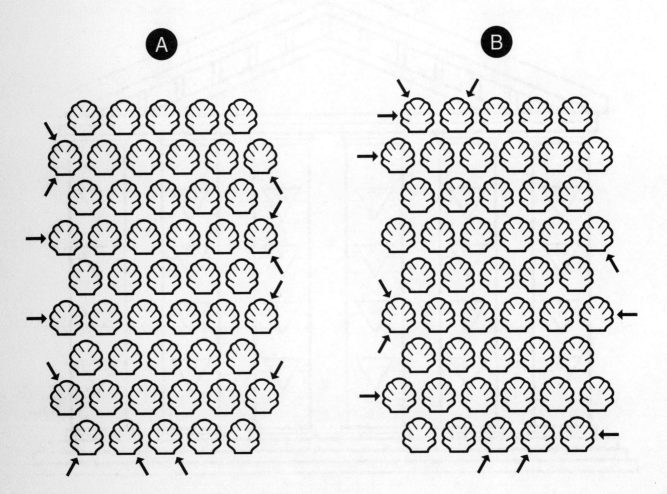

CHAIN OF BLACK SQUARES

The chain of black squares below starts at B6. Enter the next two black squares (and their connecting lines) into the diagram so that the logic system governing the black squares' positions is maintained. Neither the links nor the black squares can touch or cross.

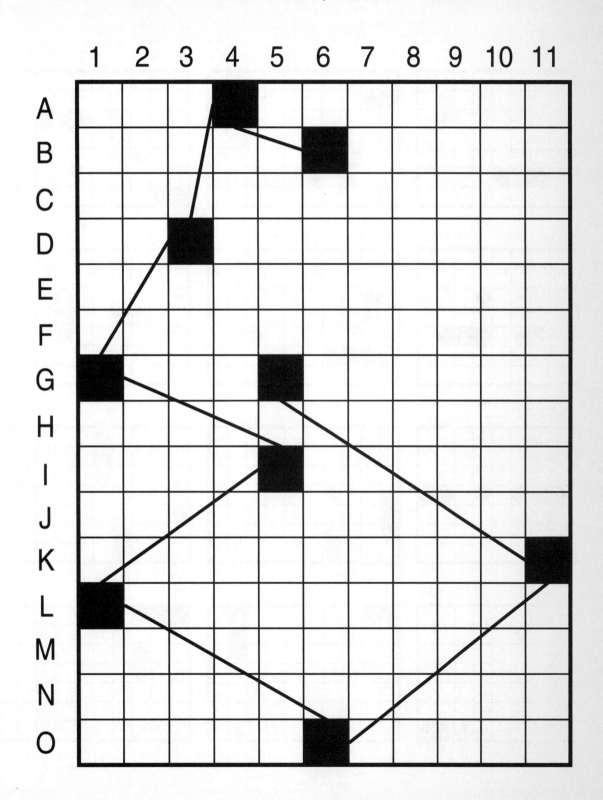

SUBMARINE IN HIDING

Each grid except the last one contains three vessels: a cruiser (3 squares), a destroyer (2 squares) and a submarine (1 square). Place the missing submarine in the last grid so its position is consistent with the governing system.

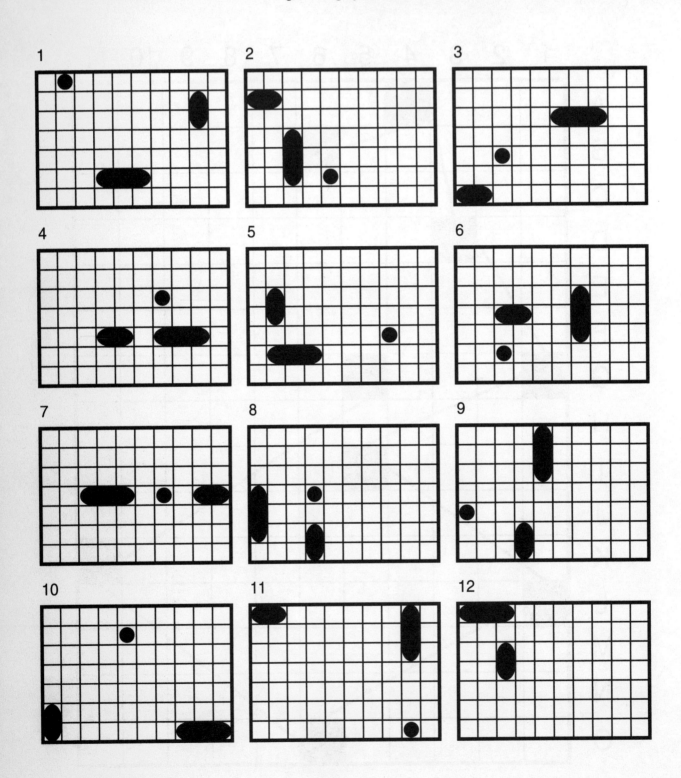

PENTHOUSES

Place the twelve penthouses (shaped like Pentominoes) into the grid so that they do not touch one another, not even diagonally. They can be rotated, but *not* reflected.
The grid includes special key symbols (illustrated below) which are to be followed in positioning the penthouses. Squares with x's must remain empty.

Pentominoes:

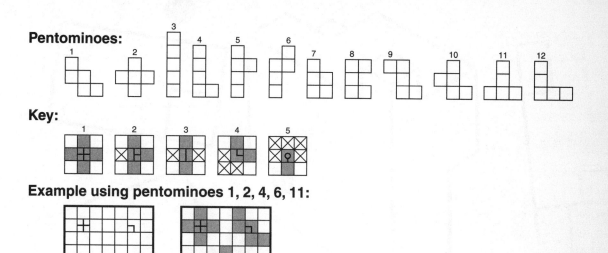

Key:

Example using pentominoes 1, 2, 4, 6, 11:

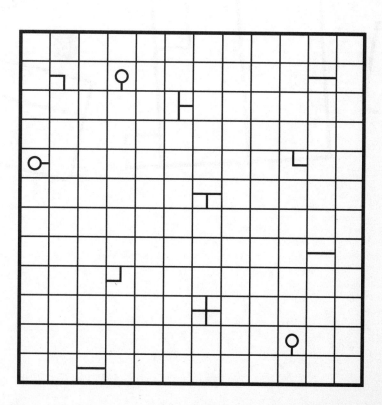

TRUE PERSPECTIVES

The solid block below is surrounded by six figures, showing the block from six points of view.
However, one perspective is drawn incorrectly. Which one?

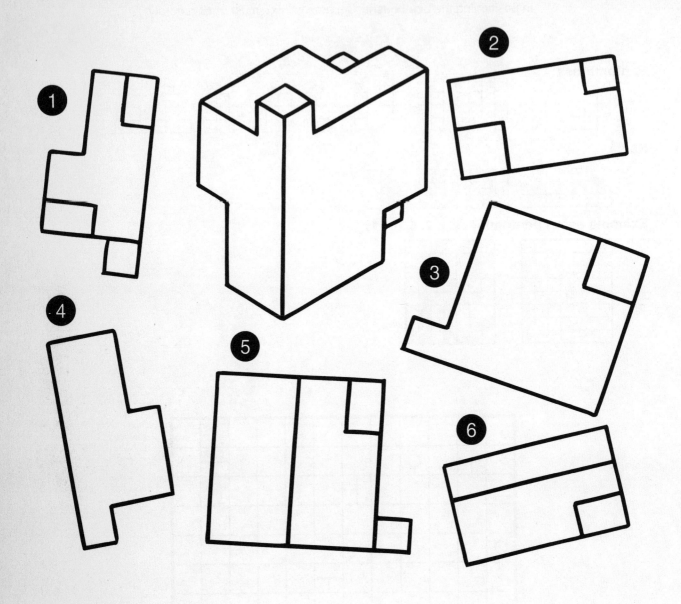

SECURITY SYSTEM

A security system is accessible using a key card with 33 possible hole positions, as illustrated below. All key cards have 16 holes. However, the "combination" that opens the lock looks at only 12 specific hole positions: any key with a subset of holes matching this unknown combination will open the lock. Of the 10 cards shows below, exactly two will open the lock. Which ones are they?

**Scheme of 33 possible
hole positions**

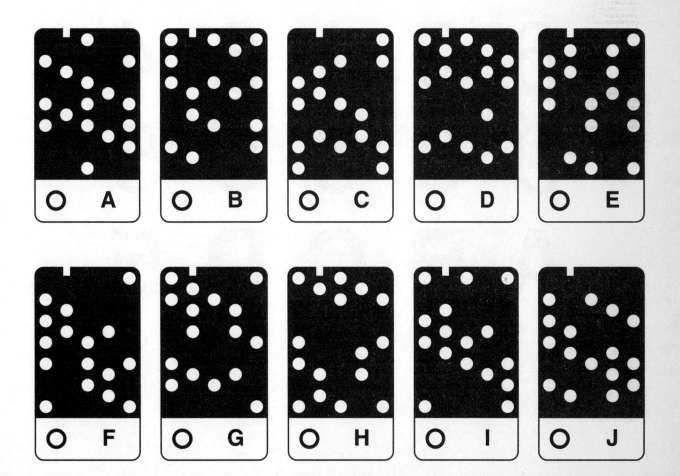

TELEPHONE NUMBERS

Below are five phone numbers created according to a certain system.
Determine the system and enter the sixth phone number in place of ABCDE.

7	3	8	2	5
7	4	0	5	9
2	4	1	7	2
6	9	1	8	4
9	3	6	8	5
A	B	C	D	E

HELLO!

On a puzzler's telephone the placement of the letters on the buttons is a bit different from the usual. The letters on each button are shown below. We are calling three famous people, one of whom is not answering. That's because he died more than 100 years ago. The second person is a popular actor; the third one was born during World War II.

1 ABC	2 DEF	3 GHI
4 JKL	5 MNO	6 PQR
7 STU	8 VWX	9 YZ

a) 5 7 1 1 6 8 3 4 2 2

b) 5 2 4 3 3 1 7 5 5

c) 6 1 7 4 7 3 5 5 5

SIGN SYSTEM

On a distant planet, ETs use a numerical system consisting of signs, each corresponding to a two-digit decimal number. Our spaceship crew decoded the message below into the 19 numbers listed, but the numbers are out of order.

To correctly recreate the message, determine the two-digit numbers that correspond to the seven signs given in the chart.

1532   ⬚⬚   3215   ⬚⬚

Sign	⬚	⬚
Number	15	32

1938
1952
1964
2374
3819
3852
3864
5219
5223
5238
6487
7423
7464
8723
8764
235287
641974
743887
873874

Sign	⬚	⬚	⬚	⬚	⬚	⬚	⬚
Number							

56

CHESS CUBES

The chess pieces on the left side of the equations represent the lengths of the sides of the cubes. The chess pieces on the right side represent the volumes of the cubes. Replace the chess pieces with digits so that in each equation the sum of the volumes of all the cubes on the left equals the volume of the cube on the right. Note: The numerical values of the chess pieces are the same for both equations.

$$2^3 + 4^3 = 72$$

$$\text{♜} = 2$$

$$\text{♛} = 4$$

$$\text{♟} = 7$$

$$\text{♟♜} = 72$$

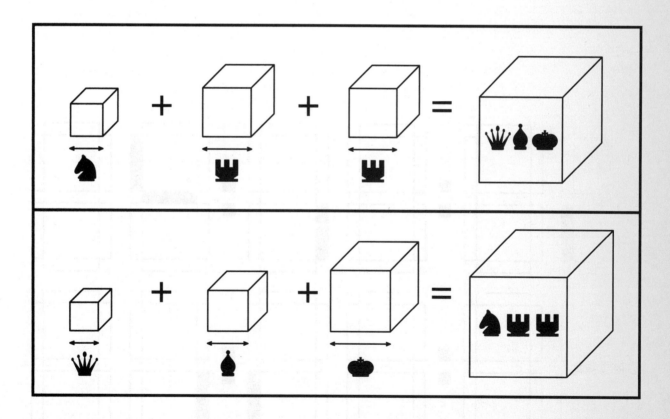

DIGITAL CLOCK

An event took exactly 131 seconds. The top picture of a 24-hour digital clock shows the time when the event began, the bottom one, when it ended. However, there was a strange breakdown and some parts of the display are not visible; the nature of the breakdown was different for the two times.
Complete the fragments to make the times correct.

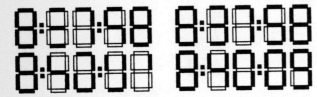

EXAMPLE

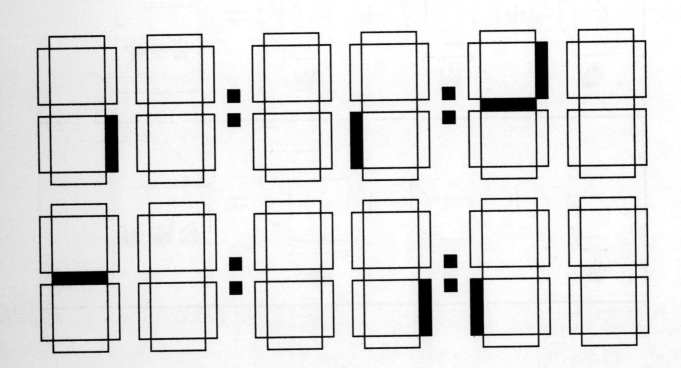

Event starting time: 8:37:58
Event ending time: 8:40:09

PUZZLE CAR

Add the logical features to the car in the center frame.

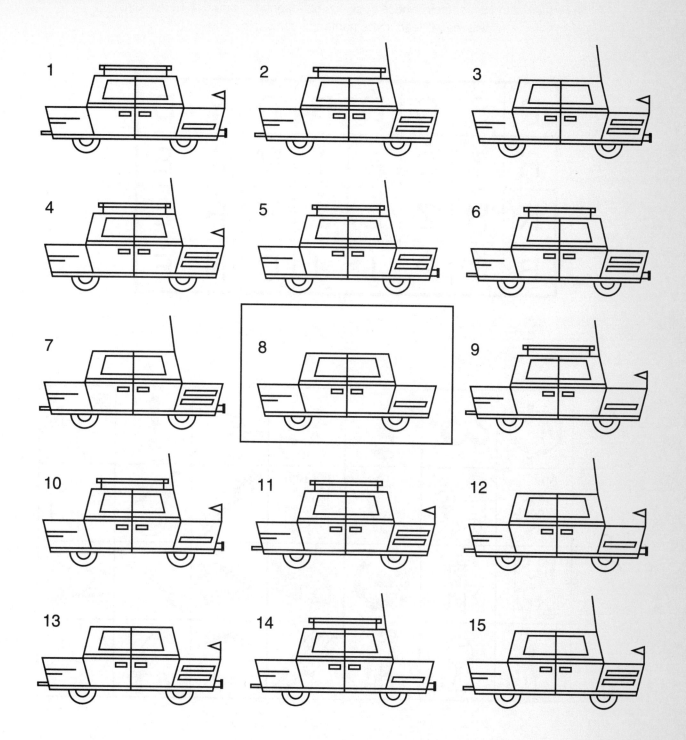

PAIRS

Cross out all the pairs of related pictures in the lower chart; some pictures will remain.
The letters in the upper chart whose positions correspond to those of the remaining
pictures will lead to the name of a famous person.

P	S	C	É	R	D	Ý	D
R	T	Š	A	I	M	Á	E
K	H	Z	L	Ž	V	Ř	L
B	Í	P	Í	J	Č	N	Ě

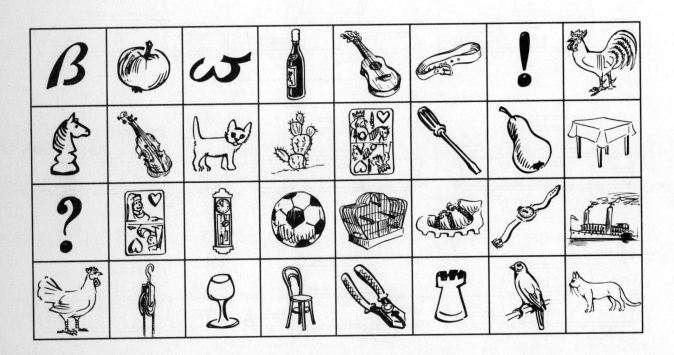

THE STAR

Fill in the empty cells so that each of the given words appears in the star diagram. Words can appear in any of the six directions shown. When you're finished, the name of another star will appear in the two framed regions; in addition, a related 6-letter word is hidden symmetrically in the diagram.

Directions

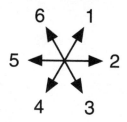

ABACUS
ABONENT
ANAPA
BASILICA
CALCIO
CARLA
ESCORT
FILLET
FORMALIN
IANUS
LABRADOR
LEOPARD
LIMPET
LISTER
MINOR
MONTEVERDI
MORAVI
NANTES
NARCIS
OILER
OTAVA
OTERO
PACKET
PAPARAZZI
SELFISH
SHAKE
SOAVE
TEMPERA
ULYSSES
VALET
VIERA
VITIS

JOIN THE CIRCLES

Join the circles with a single continuous line according to the following rules:

1. The line must proceed horizontally or vertically through the centers of the squares.
2. The line can make a 90° turn within a square.
3. No square can be re-entered (the line can neither cross nor touch itself anywhere).
4. The line must not cross squares containing letters.
5. The numbers outside the grid indicate how many squares in each column or row the line occupies, *including the two squares with circles.*

EXAMPLE

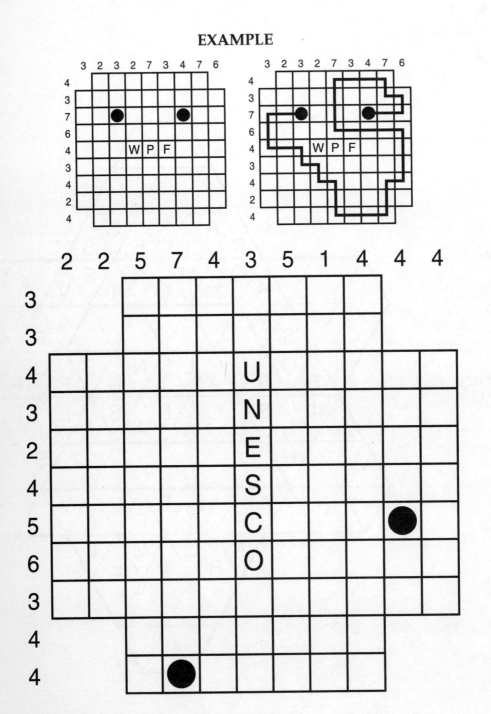

PUZZLEGRAMS

For each puzzle, place a different number from 1 to 12 into each empty space of the diagram so that the number in each circle equals the sum of the numbers in the four surrounding areas. Two numbers are already in place in each diagram.

EXAMPLE

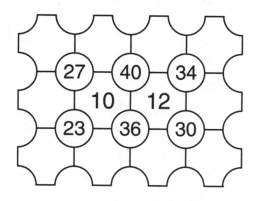

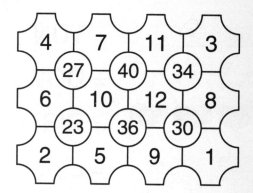

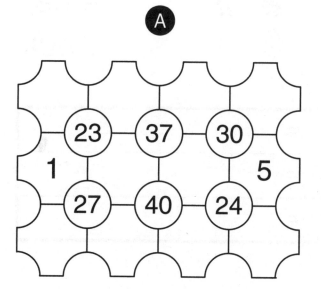

(A)

(B)

The pairs of playing card symbols and 3-letter combinations constitute a code. Using this code as the key, fill in the names of the three cities that are represented by combinations 1, 2 and 3.

♣ = LIK	♣♣♣♣ = LOS
♠♠♠ = TUN	♥ = ROK
◇◇ = DOB	♠ = TIK
♥♥♥♥ = RIS	◇◇◇◇ = DUS
♣♣ = LUB	♥♥♥ = RON
♠♠♠♠ = TOS	♣♣♣ = LUN
♦♦♦ = DIN	♠♠ = TIB
♥♥ = RUB	◇ = DUK

1	♠ ♠ ♥	=
2	♣ ♣ ♣ ◇ ◇ ◇	=
3	◇ ◇ ♣ ♣ ♣	=

GARDENS

Each of the grids below contains several gardens (solid white areas) separated by a continuous path of black squares. The size of each garden (its total number of white squares) is given in one of its squares. Neighboring gardens may touch each other either at their corners or not at all. The black path must be a single unbroken area. It may branch, but it may not include areas that are 2 x 2 squares. Gardens may be any shape. Determine the layout of all the gardens and the path in each puzzle.

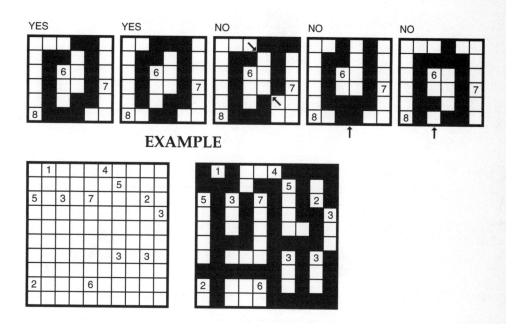

EXAMPLE

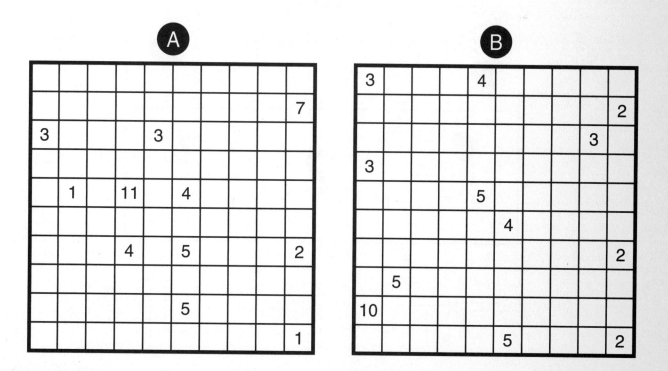

CORNERS

Replace the question mark with the appropriate corner.
First select the corner with the correct shape and position from the choices at the bottom.
Then draw the black and lined parts in their correct positions on that corner.

EXAMPLE

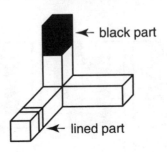

← black part

← lined part

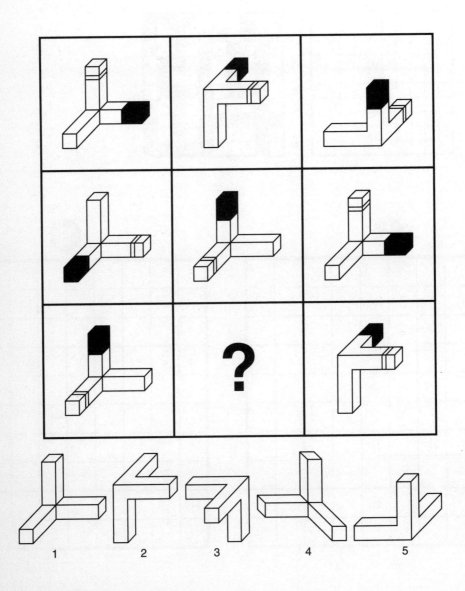

NOBEL BALLS

From four channels holding 30 balls, individual balls with letters are released one at a time. Each ball will slide down the sloping plane and drop into the first free vertical column (1). When the column is completely filled with five balls, the next five balls released will drop into the second column (2), etc, until all six columns are completely filled. The balls must be released from the channels in such a way that the names of six of the Nobel prizewinners listed below are spelled out reading down each column. Two consecutive balls may not be released from the same channel.

EXAMPLE

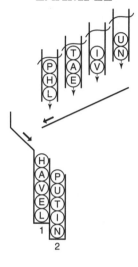

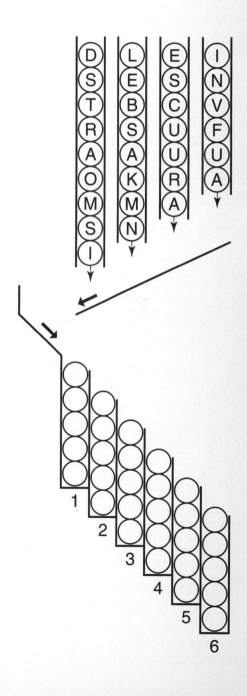

ASTON	FERMI
BASOV	FUKUI
BRAUN	FRANK
BUNIN	KREBS
CAMUS	MINOT
CURIE	RAMAN
DIELS	RUSKA
DIRAC	SALAM
ELIOT	SIMON
ERNST	STERN

SPELLED-OUT MATH

Replace the letters with numbers as in a cryptogram so that the indicated total is correct and so that the given constraint is satisfied. (Every letter represents the same number throughout.)

EXAMPLE
N is less than 5 (N < 5)

```
    T W O              1 0 6
  T H R E E          1 9 7 2 2
  S E V E N          8 2 5 2 4
  ---------        ---------
  T W E L V E      1 0 2 3 5 2
```

S is greater than 6 (S > 6)

```
          T W O
  S E V E N
  E L E V E N
  -----------
  T W E N T Y
```

DICEY DICE

Fill in the pips on the last die so that the logic of the sequence is maintained.

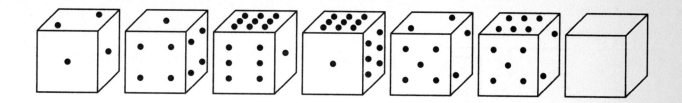

NUMERICAL PROGRESSION

Supply the missing number in the numerical progression.

SHIFTS

Put the numbers in numerical order using 12 moves. A move consists of shifting a number from its current position into the empty spot. Shifts between the nine positions are only carried out along the marked tracks. After 12 moves, the empty spot must be at the end of the numerical succession.

EXAMPLE   **Moves: 3,1,3**

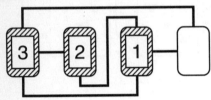

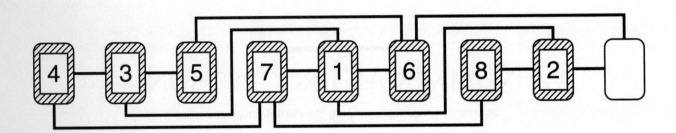

CUBIC BATTLESHIPS

These cubic navy battles are played like classic Battleships, but the "water" consists of three visible sides of a cube. Vessels can be placed on one cube face or can wrap around the cube edges. They cannot border on one another, not even diagonally. The numbers on the sides of each grid indicate the total number of ship segments in the three directions indicated. The X in the second puzzle indicates that that cell cannot contain a ship segment.

Tracks:

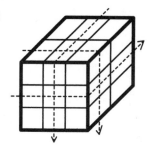

EXAMPLE

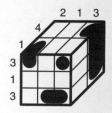

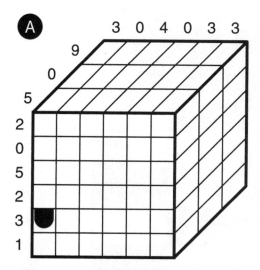

A

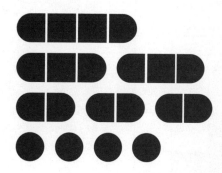

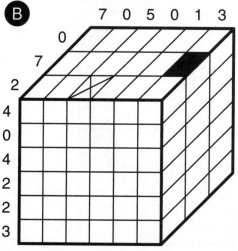

B

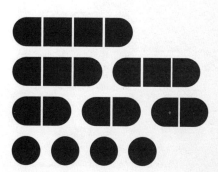

71

DAYS ON END

Enter each of the days of the week, MONDAY, TUESDAY, WEDNESDAY, THURSDAY, FRIDAY, SATURDAY and SUNDAY, one or more times into the grid below. They should be written one after another, reading from left to right down the diagram; however, they do not have to be in calendar succession. No square can be left empty and the same letter cannot appear more than once in a row or column. Two letters have been entered to start you off.

EXAMPLE (partially filled in)

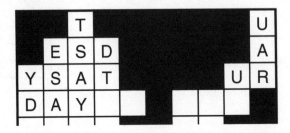

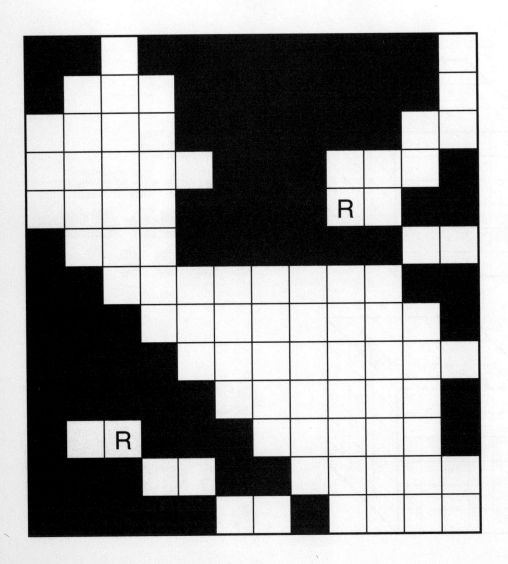

Do You Play Handball?

The scores of four matches of a handball tournament are given below. How many points did the VARTA TALLIN team score in the fifth match? Which well-known personality will help you to determine the answer?

AMORO PRAGUE   23—31   VARTA TALLIN
LIRA BRNO   23—23   MARS DENVER
MARS DENVER   24—43   AMORO PRAGUE
VARTA TALLIN   45—14   LIRA BRNO

VARTA TALLIN   ??

MAGIC CALCULATION

Place the numbers from 1 to 25 into the 25 boxes A–Y so that the results of the indicated arithmetic operations between adjoining boxes are correct horizontally and vertically. The arithmetic operations, given inside the circles, are: addition (+), subtraction (–), multiplication (x) and division (:). In some cases, the numbers in the circles have been replaced with letters; each of these letters represents the numerical value of the corresponding box.

EXAMPLE

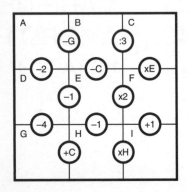 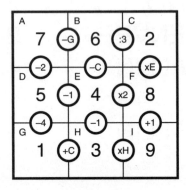

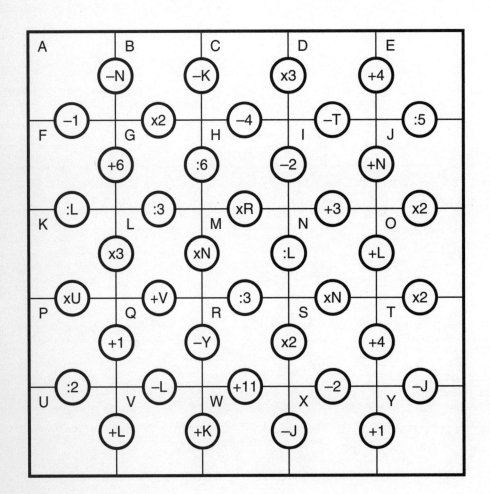

SITE AND PLOTS

The site is divided into ten rectangular plots, each with a different survey number from 1 to 10. The total for a plot is the sum of the survey numbers of the adjacent plots, not including the plot's own survey number. Place the survey numbers into the ten circles.

EXAMPLE

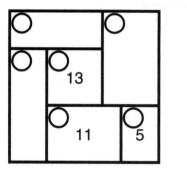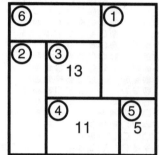

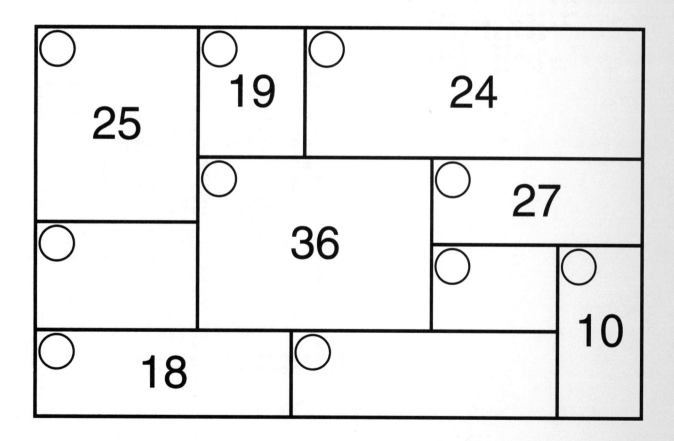

FAT SQUIRRELS

Find the ten differences between these two pictures.

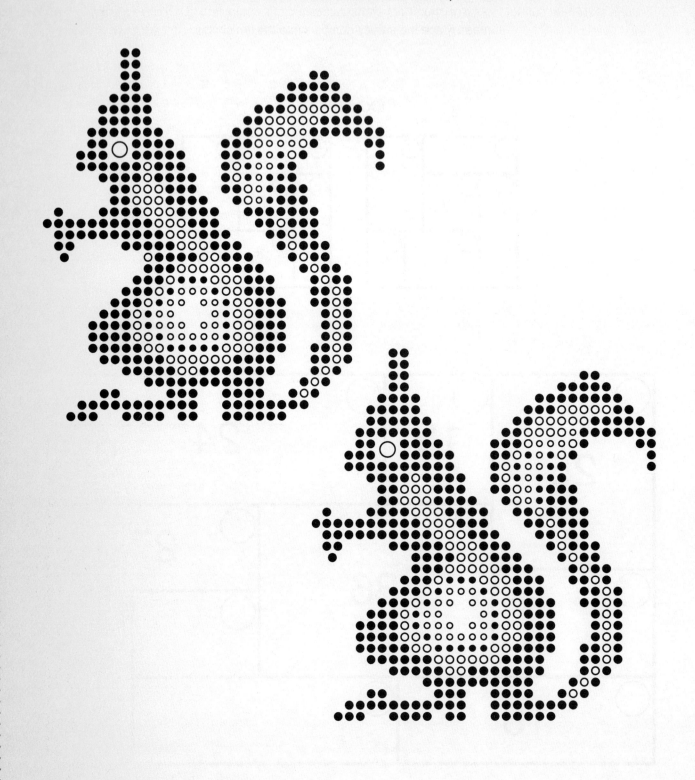

MAGNETS

In each puzzle, the diagram is made up of magnetic and non-magnetic plates. Each magnetic plate has two halves: positive (+) and negative (–). The halves with the same charge cannot touch each other, since they repel each other (however, their corners can touch). The numbers of positive and negative charges in each row and column are marked. One magnetic plate has already been placed in each diagram. Mark the position of all the magnetic plates in the diagram. Non-magnetic insulation plates are the same size as the magnetic ones and are to be marked in black.

EXAMPLE

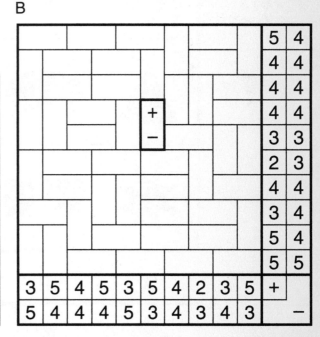

INFINITE LINE

An infinite sequence is made up of a repeating pattern of six different symbols. In each of the first five lines, four symbols are given in the correct order, but in each case one or two symbols are omitted.

Line six follows the same rule but with one exception: two of the symbols are in the wrong position. Which two symbols must be swapped so that line six follows the original rule?

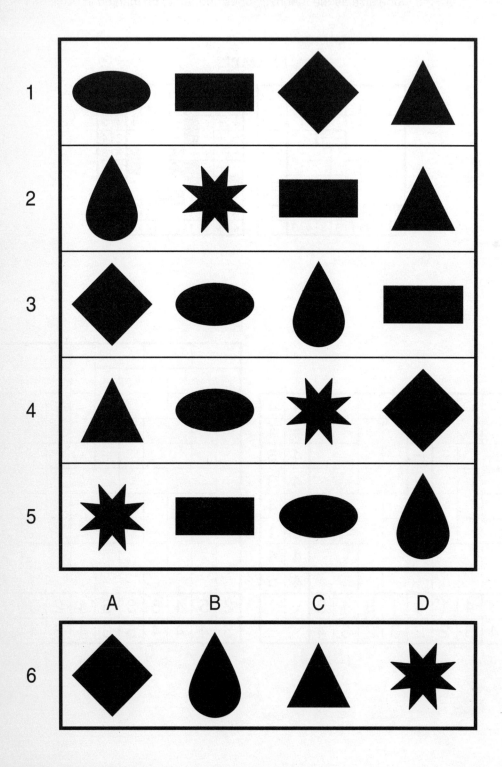

MAGIC ATOMIUM

Enter a different number from 1 to 16 into each circle so that the sum of the four circled numbers in each of the following locations is 34:

- on each of the eight oblique abscissas of the diagram
- on each of its 2 marked diagonals
- on the corners of each of the nine small squares
- on the circle
- on each of the two ellipses

Four of the numbers have already been entered.

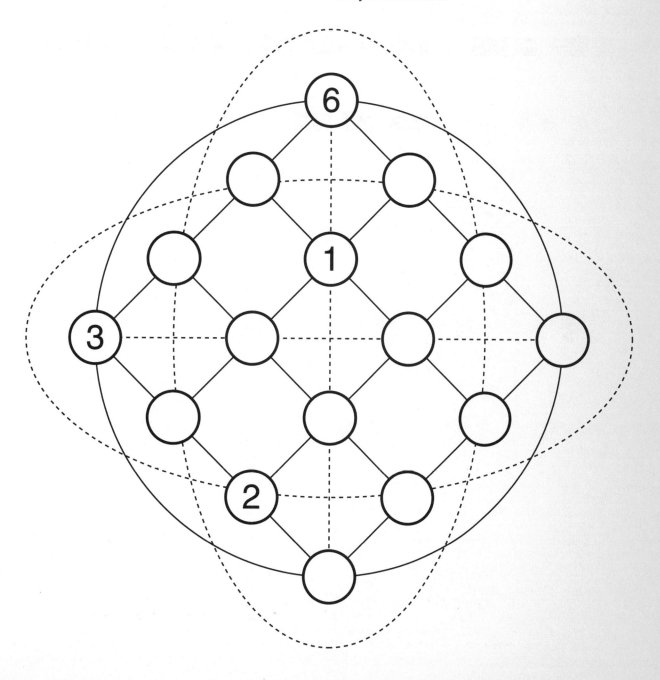

SOS

Replace the question mark with the correct combination of dots and dashes.

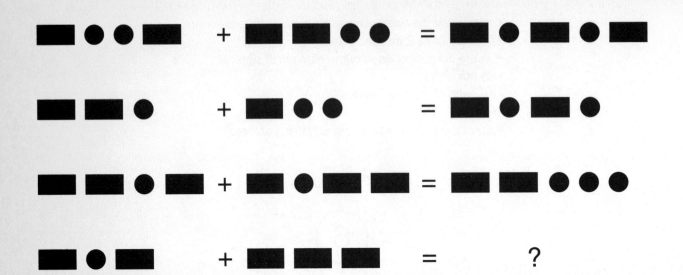

CONSTRUCTION SITE

For each puzzle, a crane operator must systematically transfer all of the numbered panels to the container on the left so that they fit completely and are flat on top. From the heap, the operator can only load a free panel—that is, one that can be pulled straight upwards. The operator then drops the panel into the container in the same orientation and must not move it again. Black areas are blocks preventing the collapse of the heap and are not transferred to the container. Each container already contains one correctly placed panel.

EXAMPLE

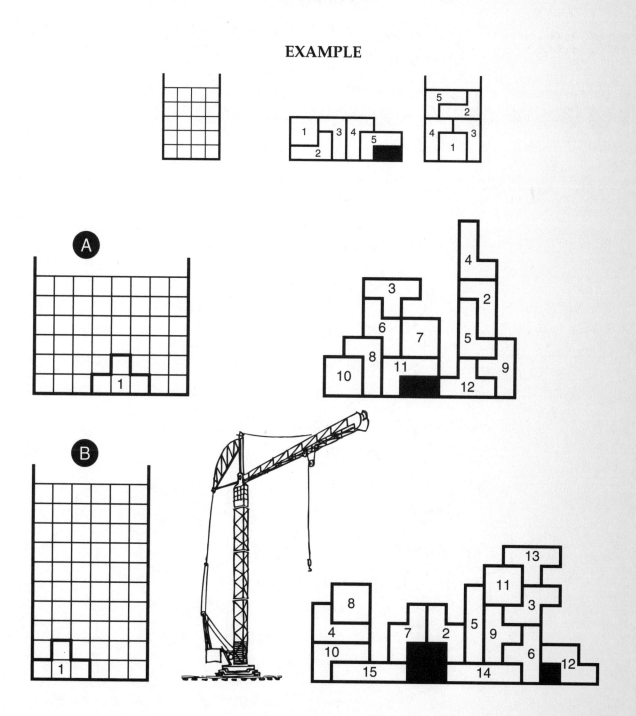

HONEYCOMB

For each puzzle, place each of the numbers from 1 to 10 into the diagram exactly once so that every line in every direction contains two numbers. The sums of the 15 pairs of numbers must all be different.

EXAMPLE

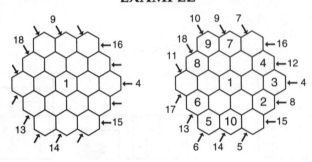

A

B

C

ROTATING HONEYCOMB

Numbers have been placed in the circles of the honeycombs. When honeycombs are rotated clockwise and counterclockwise, the positions of the numbers change. Turn two honeycombs so that the total of the numbers in each of the four honeycombs is identical.
The example is meant to illustrate only how the honeycombs move.

Examples of Rotation

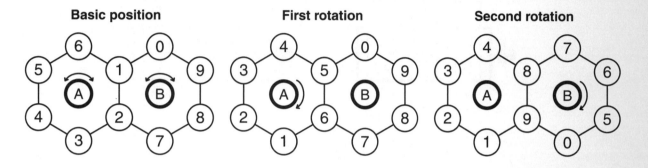

Basic position   First rotation   Second rotation

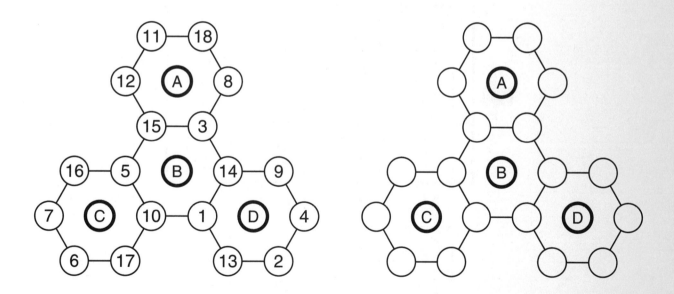

UP AND DOWN

The four columns below are all even so far—but only so far. Your task is to move any or all of the columns upward or downward so that you can read a meaningful continuous text of 16 letters in the framed area.

EXAMPLE

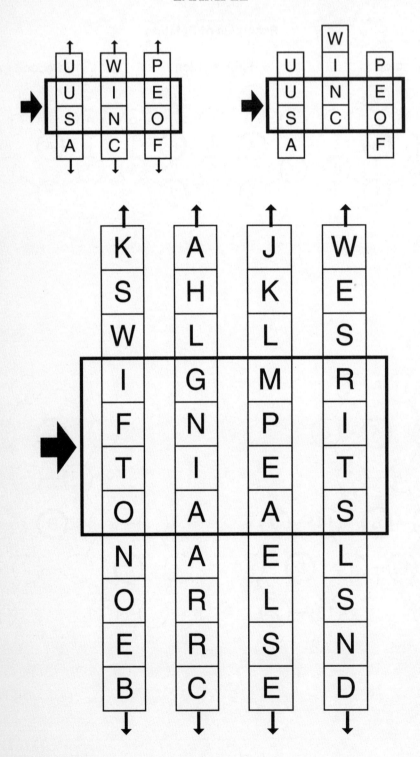

A PATH BETWEEN CELLS

For each puzzle below, draw a line along the edges of the cells to form a continuous route.
The number inside a given cell indicates how many of its edges are part of the route.

EXAMPLE

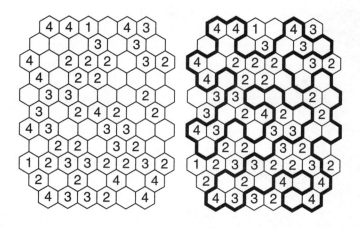

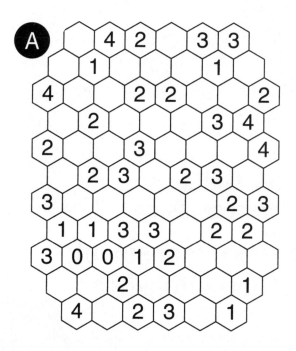

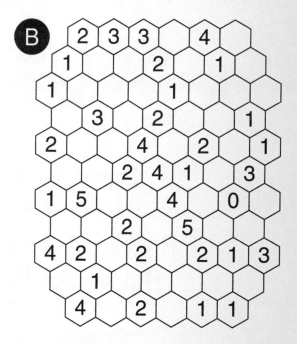

ANSWERS

2001 Qualifying Test
Point Values

Page/Puzzle		Points
7.	Great Divide	5 points
7.	Number Boxes	10 points
8.	Birdie for the Bear	5 points
9.	Common Touch	5 points each
	+ 5 bonus points for all three	
10.	Missing Dominoes	5 points
11.	Domino Stacking	10 points
12.	Crisscross	10 points
13.	Battleships	10 points
14.	End View	15 points
15.	Sum Place	10 points
15.	Loop-D-Loop	15 points
16.	Club Sandwich	20 points
17.	Railroad Tracks	15 points
18.	50/50 Minesweeper	10 points
19.	Alice Maze	25 points
20.	Cross Sums Variation	20 points
21.	Bad Math	15 points
22.	Retrograde Battleships	15 points
22.	Totally Battleships	10 points
23.	Have Sum Fun!	15 points
23.	High Five	10 points
24.	Arrowheading	15 points
25.	Meandering River	30 points
26.	Fences Variation	30 points

7. Great Divide

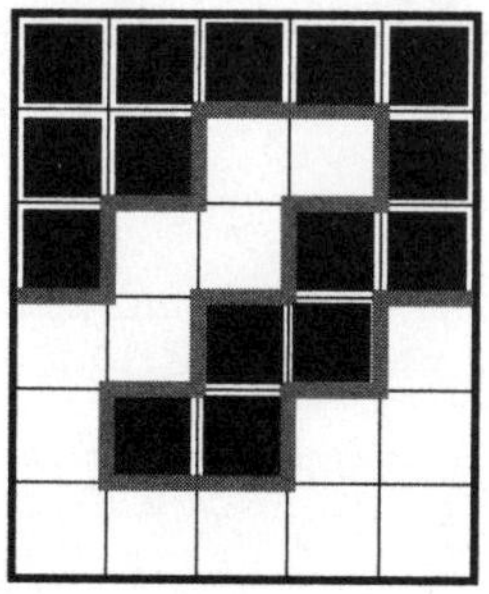

7. Number Boxes

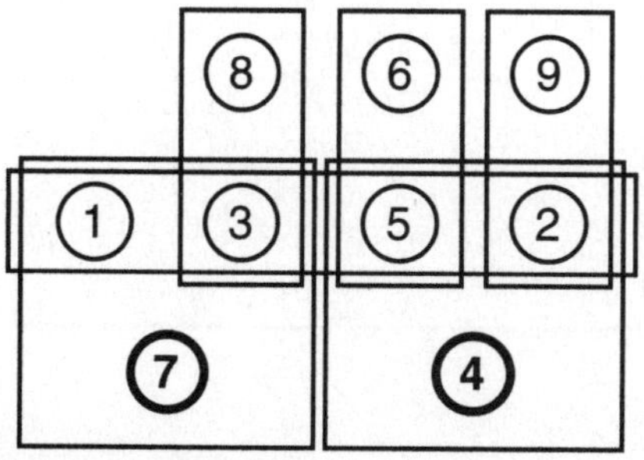

8. Birdie for the Bear

4

9. Common Touch

1. Stowe, United States (city ends with long "o" sound)
2. Alma-Ata, Kazakhstan (last letter of city is 2nd and 4th letter of country)
3. Chinju, Korea (all five vowels appear just once)

10. Missing Dominoes

3–3; 5–5

11. Domino Stacking

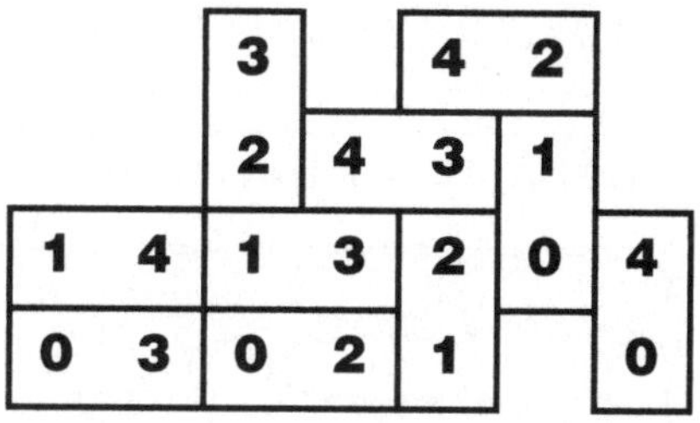

12. Crisscross

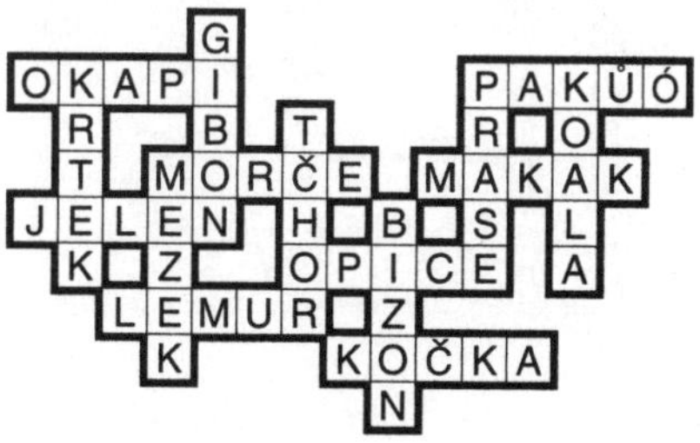

The missing animal is Bůvol

13. Battleships

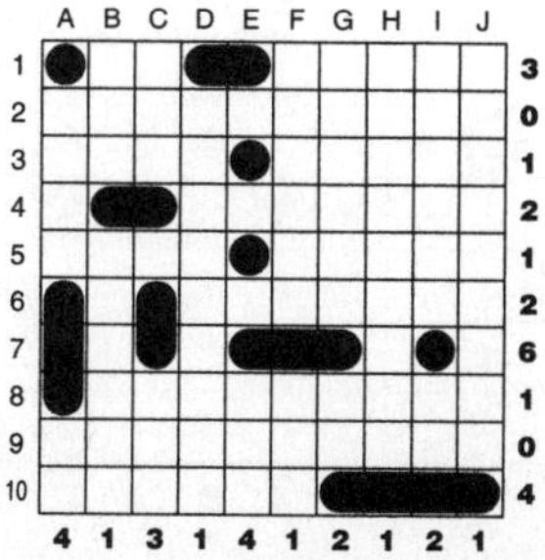

14. End View

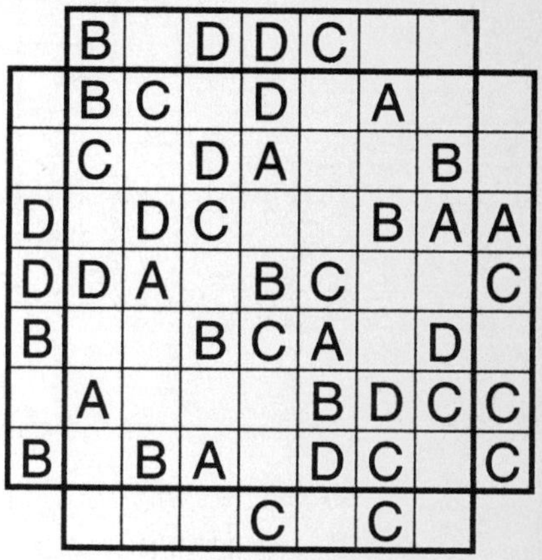

15. Sum Place

9 (the number of distinct letters in both country names)

15. Loop-D-Loop

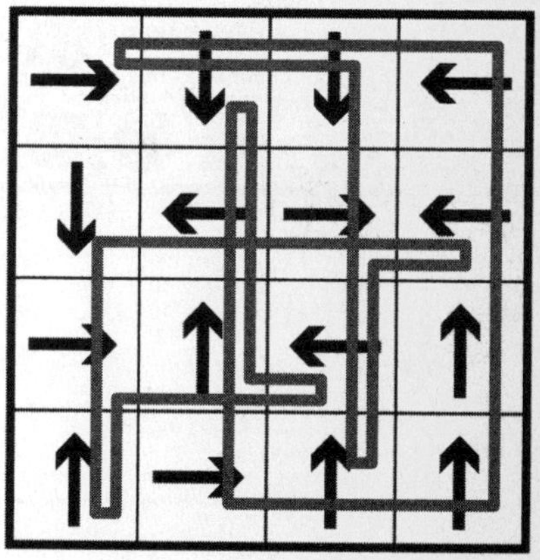

16. Club Sandwich

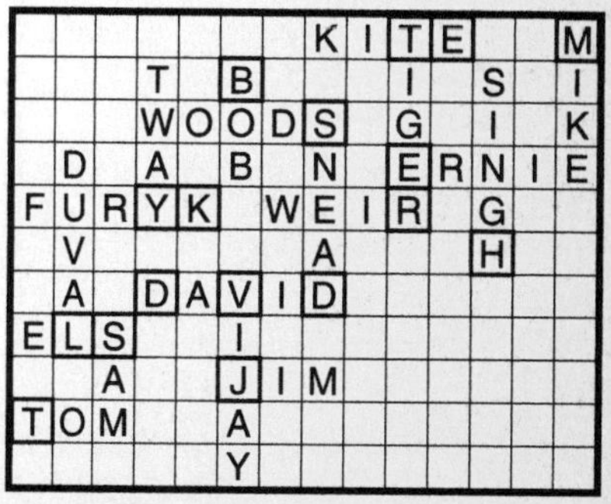

17. RAILROAD TRACKS

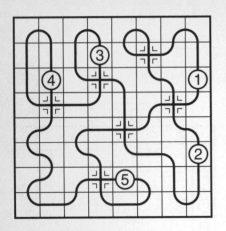

18. 50/50 MINESWEEPER

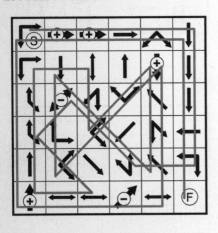

19. ALICE MAZE

20. CROSS SUMS VARIATION

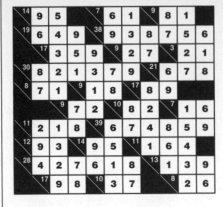

21. BAD MATH

$$
\begin{array}{r}
1033 \\
31\overline{)32023} \\
\underline{31} \\
102 \\
\underline{93} \\
93 \\
\underline{93} \\
93
\end{array}
$$

22. RETROGRADE BATTLESHIPS

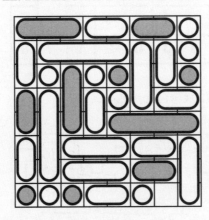

22. TOTALLY BATTLESHIPS

5	5	5	7	5	9	1	7	3	1	**1**
9	9	9	9	4	5	3	3	4	2	**3**
6	7	8	7	5	5	9	6	6	4	**30**
9	2	7	5	9	5	7	7	7	3	**9**
6	2		5	5	1	1	4	8	6	**20**
5	5	5	5	3	1	2	2	8	8	**5**
7	6	4	4	8	1	3	3	9	1	**15**
2	5	8	1	3	8	1	1	8	2	**5**
6	9	4	5	6	3	5	9	4	3	**3**
7	5	9	2	8	4	5	1	4	1	**4**
15	**5**	**13**	**7**	**5**	**4**	**8**	**7**	**27**	**4**	

23. HAVE SUM FUN!

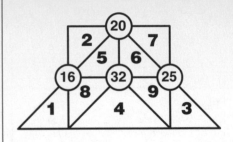

23. HIGH FIVE

−3, 3, 9, 14, 23

24. ARROWHEADING

ARROWHEAD-INGS

24

25. MEANDERING RIVER

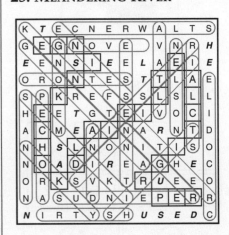

26. FENCES VARIATION

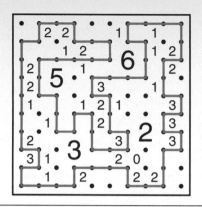

28. WELCOME TO BRNO!

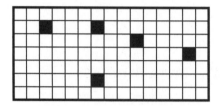

All 8 overlaid:

29. FIND THE DOGS

A

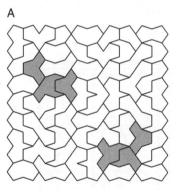

B

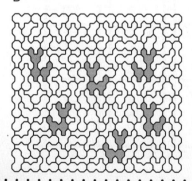

30. STAR TOURS

Atlas–C　　　Meres–A
Botein–K　　Polaris–H
Coxa–J　　　Rigel–I
Deneb–L　　Subra–B
Furud–D　　Toliman–E
Kuma–G　　　Vega–F

31. DISTANT FUTURE

JOHN:　4987
ALES:　5012
ALDY:　5036

31. MULTIPLICATION

345 x 986 = 340,170

32. WORMS

A

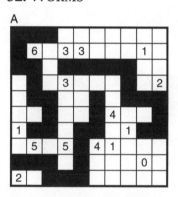

B

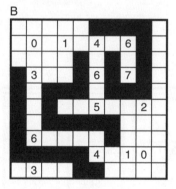

33. NAMES IN A TELESCOPE

Carme, Elara, Metis, Thebe

34. SPACESHIP

Picture A is the original.

35. INVASION

A

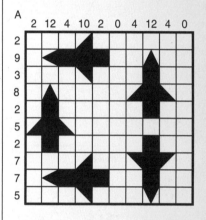

B

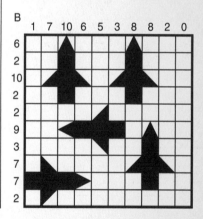

36. ASTEROIDS

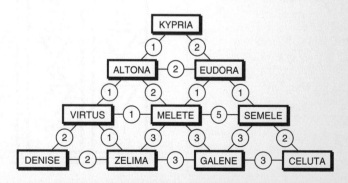

37. CONSTELLATION

24—The value of a small star is the sum of the connecting segments; the value of a large star is twice the sum of the connecting segments. The value of a constellation is the sum of the values of its stars.

38. MISSION

B, C, D

39. TETRAHEDRON 2001

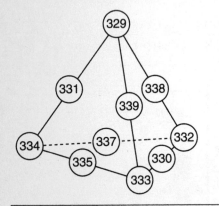

40. DIVIDE THE AREA

41. ANTIMAGIC SQUARE

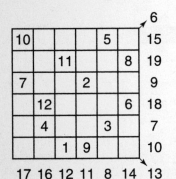

42. FOUR MARKSMEN

All four marksmen scored 21 points. Adams: 3, 5, 13; Bernard: 2, 9, 10; Clinton: 1, 8, 12; Davis: 4, 6, 11

43. SYMBOLIC WOMEN

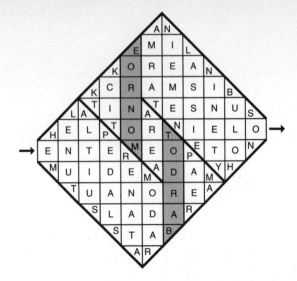

Monroe; Bardot

44. UMBRELLAS

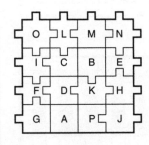

B3   C2

45. LETTER BLOCKS

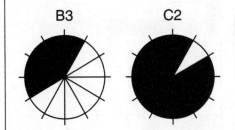

46. EXCHANGES

A2 ⟷ A4
D2 ⟷ D5

47. COLUMNS

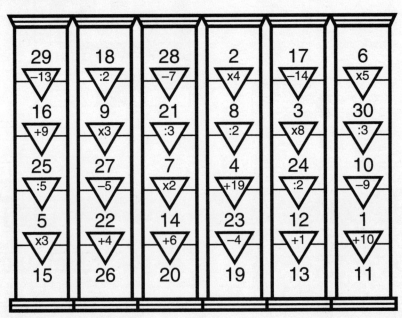

48. PEARLS

A

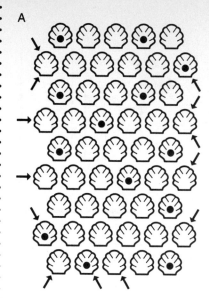

B

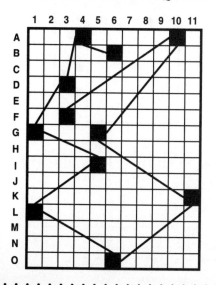

49. CHAIN OF BLACK SQUARES

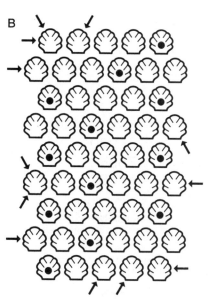

50. SUBMARINE IN HIDING

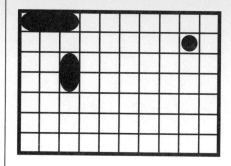

51. PENTHOUSES

52. TRUE PERSPECTIVES

6

53. SECURITY SYSTEM

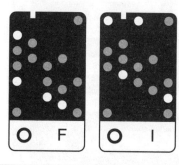

54. TELEPHONE NUMBERS

1 6 0 3 5

55. HELLO!

a) Oscar Wilde
b) Mel Gibson
c) Paul Simon

56. SIGN SYSTEM

| 52 | 23 | 64 | 87 | 74 | 19 | 38 |

57. CHESS CUBES

♛ = 1

♞ = 2

♝ = 3

♜ = 4

♚ = 6

♛♝♚ = 136

♞♛♜ = 244

58. DIGITAL CLOCK

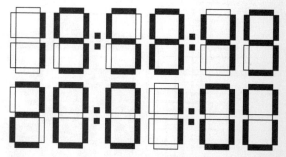

Start: 19:58:49
End: 20:01:00

59. Puzzle Car

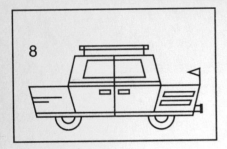

60. Pairs

DALI

61. The Star

Outlined areas: Luciano Pavarotti
Six "points" reading clockwise from
bottom: Italia

62. Join the Circles

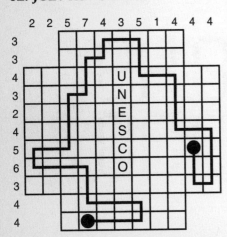

63. Puzzlegrams

A

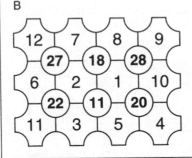

B

64. Card Code

1. Tobruk
2. London
3. Dublin

65. Gardens

A

B

66. Corners

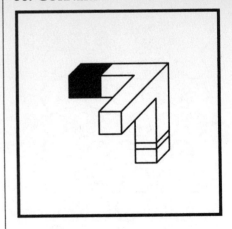

67. Nobel Balls

1. RAMAN
2. FUKUI
3. CAMUS
4. BASOV
5. STERN
6. DIELS

68. Spelled-Out Math

930
78682
858682

938294

69. Dicey Dice

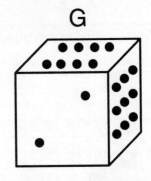

69. Numerical Progression

204 (= 35 × 6 − 6)

70. Shifts

6, 5, 3, 1, 2, 8, 7, 4, 1, 2, 5, 6

71. CUBIC BATTLESHIPS

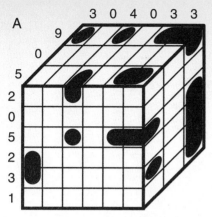

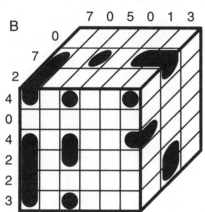

74. MAGIC CALCULATION

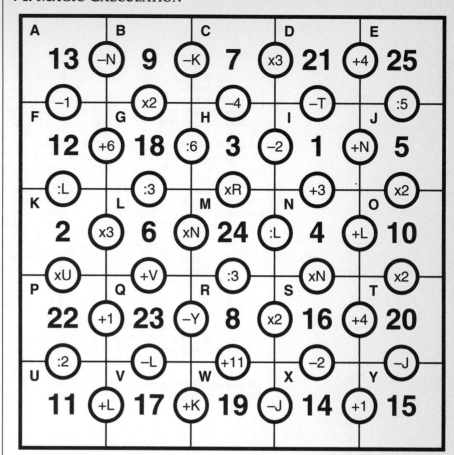

72. DAYS ON END

73. DO YOU PLAY HANDBALL?

The two digits of each score indicate letters in the corresponding first and last names of the teams. VARTA TALLIN goals: 12. Name of the personality: The resulting letters spell Martina Navratilova.

75. SITE AND PLOTS

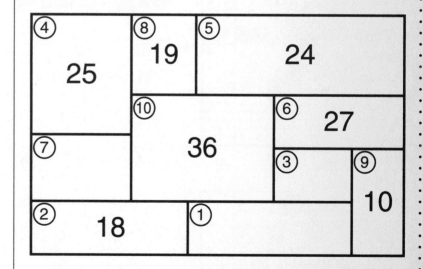

76. Fat Squirrels

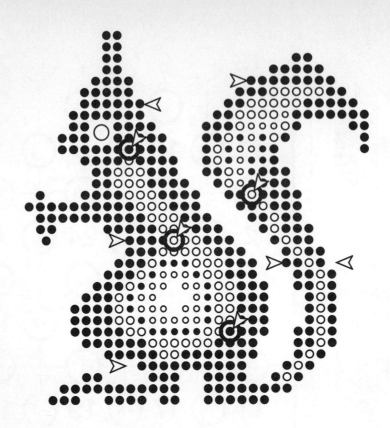

77. Magnets

A

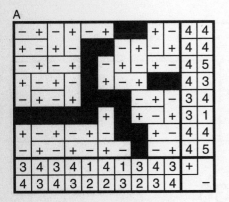

B

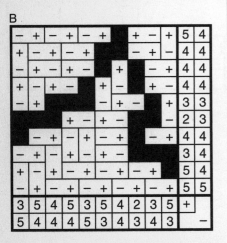

78. Infinite Line

6. A C B D

79. Magic Atomium

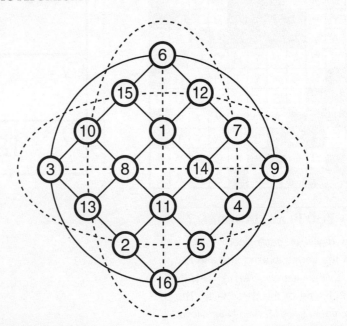

94

80. SOS

? = ▬ ▬ ● ●

81. CONSTRUCTION SITE

A

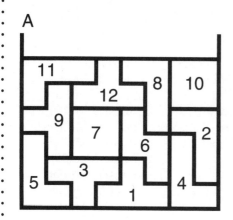

B

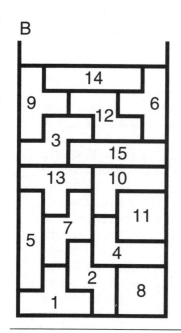

82. HONEYCOMB

A

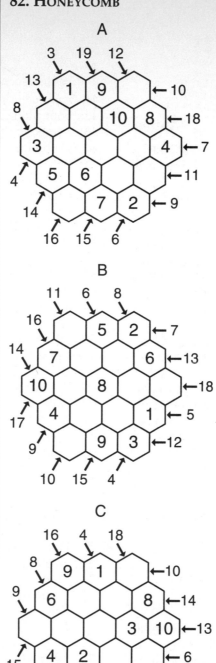

B

C

83. ROTATING HONEYCOMB

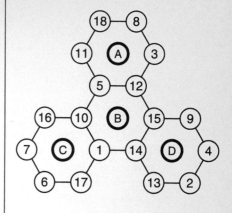

84. UP AND DOWN
THE ROLLING STONES

85. A PATH BETWEEN CELLS

A

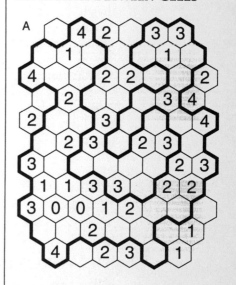

B

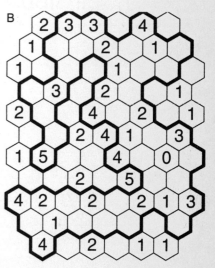

CREDITS